IMAGES OF LONDON

HARINGEY
AT WAR

October 2004

Tony,
It's hot off the press.
Happy Birthday
Love Rob

IMAGES OF LONDON

HARINGEY
AT WAR

DEBORAH HEDGECOCK
AND ROBERT WAITE

TEMPUS

Frontispiece: Major E. Thorold Garland of the Royal Engineers in September 1916. He was Chairman of Tottenham Council from 1907 to 1908 and from 1915 to 1916.

First published 2004

Tempus Publishing Limited
The Mill, Brimscombe Port,
Stroud, Gloucestershire, GL5 2QG
www.tempus-publishing.com

British Library Cataloguing in Publication Data.
A catalogue record for this book is available from the British Library.

ISBN 0 7524 3297 4

Typesetting and origination by Tempus Publishing Limited.
Printed in Great Britain.

Contents

Acknowledgements

This book was inspired by the important collection of photographs and oral histories at Bruce Castle Museum that tell the poignant and moving stories of the lives of Haringey people during the two World Wars in the twentieth century. We are most grateful to those individuals – some anonymous, others unknown – who have generously donated or loaned cherished family photographs for inclusion in this work and as additions to the museum's collections. In particular we thank Eunice Barber, Daphne Bradley, Pauline Charles, Iris and Alf Church, Stanley Cohen, Freda Croucher, Charles Edwards, Henry Jacobs, Len O'Flanagan, Alan Read, Vera Redwin, David Smith, Monica Smith and Joan Thompson. We apologise to any we have omitted.

We would not have been able to write this book without the invaluable knowledge and information from local historians and residents. Thank you to Lee Arnot, Alan Barker, Ken Barker, Gladys Brandon, Irene Broadly, Peter Calvert, Sylvia Collicott, Coombes Croft Reminiscence Group, Pat Cryer, the Friends of Bruce Castle, Margarite Day, Ken Gay, Mick Geoghegan, Oona Kelly, Jim Lewis, Albert Pinching, Chris Protz, Cathy Redman, Charlie Rolland, Bill Rust, Joan Schwitzer and Alan and Ray Swain. For their kindness, support and hard work we thank the staff at Bruce Castle Museum: Libby Adams, Trevor Bryan, Rhiannon Cackett, Jeff Gerhardt, Gigi Guizzo, George Ioannou, Rita and Alan Read and Chris Rice. Our particular thanks is owed to Janet Harris and Hazel Whitehouse – we are greatly indebted to you both.

If readers would like to donate original photographs to be added to the borough's historical collections or lend original photographs for copying, please contact the curator at Bruce Castle Museum (Lordship Lane, London N17 8NU) or on 020 8808 8772.

Introduction

This book looks at the impact of the two World Wars on Haringey through rare and personal photographs and people's memories. Such wartime images are all the more unique given the low production and cost of photographic film in the early years of the twentieth century. The pursuit of photography was yet to become the popular hobby that it is today. In Edwardian Britain, cameras were expensive and amateur photography was unusual; it was largely confined to those who had the means to indulge this interest.

By the time of the Second World War in 1939, photography was more commonplace but still not yet an everyday family pastime. Among the many products rationed during the Second World War was photographic film. In addition, the taking of pictures was highly restricted in the interests of national security. This remarkable collection of photographs from Bruce Castle Museum offers an important pictorial record of the wartime history of the London borough of Haringey, highlighting not only important events for the former boroughs of Tottenham, Hornsey and Wood Green, but life-changing events for its residents.

At the beginning of the twentieth century the passing of the Victorian era saw little change in the cherished values of people living in Tottenham, Hornsey and Wood Green (collectively known today as Haringey). These recently formed suburbs of London continued to thrive whilst the country established itself as the greatest military and industrial power in the world. As Germany emerged as a strong military threat, a major war became impossible to avoid. When war was declared in Europe on 4 August 1914, Haringey responded immediately – but life was never going to be the same again. A strong sense of patriotic duty moved men to go off to fight for their country. The Middlesex Regiment, formed in 1881, absorbed many of the local volunteers. Of those who served in France during the First World War, very few survived. Local manufacturers in Tottenham Hale turned their hand to the demand for mass-production of munitions, keeping the armed forces supplied with military hardware. Women took the place of their men-folk in the workplace – in factories, transport and on the land.

In one way or another, the war came home to everyone. Nothing before could have prepared people for the sheer scale of human sacrifice that would be the hallmark of the 'Great War'. Tens of thousands of young men who had answered their country's call to arms were ordered to advance on the battlefield against overwhelming German artillery. Many who had grown up in Haringey would never return to their family and friends.

With the First World War came the horror of new technology. In the trenches, troops were surrounded by the bloody carnage caused by machine guns, bombs and poisonous gas attacks. Back home, as with many boroughs, air-raids in Haringey were a new experience of hostility and was one that would develop further in future conflict.

Refugees from the German invasion of Belgium also arrived in Britain with the outbreak of war. Locally, Alexandra Palace played a key role in Britain's response to this national aid relief, having been requisitioned to provide temporary shelter for the refugees. With the widespread anti-German riots across London, the Palace was used again to intern German civilians living in this country.

The war, that at first people were led to believe would be 'over by Christmas', lasted four years. Germany surrendered unconditionally in 1918 but the foundations of the next great conflict were laid almost immediately. The people of Haringey rallied to pick up the pieces of normal life as they mourned their many dead and continued to care for its wounded.

Enduring their share of unemployment in the economic slump of the 1920s, these years proved particularly hard for working people and their families in Haringey. The 1930s turned a corner for Haringey – there was a mass clearance of slum dwellings and newer housing stock built by the London County Council in the form of 'cottage' estates providing better accommodation for the poor. Although the last of Haringey's farms were lost to make way for the housing, the nursery industry in the Lea Valley flourished as did local manufacturing businesses in Tottenham and Wood Green.

During this time, the Nazi regime gained power in Germany. In Britain, Oswald Mosley whipped his fascist followers into a frenzy at street rallies. The threat of fascist persecution endangered the lives of members of the large Jewish community in Haringey.

When Germany invaded Poland on 1 September 1939, Britain once again found itself at war. With the horrific memories of the 1914-1918 conflict still raw in people's minds, residents of Haringey, like the rest of the country, had little appetite for war. Listening to the skilful oratory of Winston Churchill, however, people began to realise they would have to fight for their very existence. Civil Defence operations had been well underway in Haringey for two years before war was declared. Another year of practising Air-Raid Precautions would pass before bombing raids began.

All attention was focussed on winning and thousands volunteered to enlist in the armed forces. On the home front, the country looked to initiatives from Haringey to make Britain's domestic economy both highly efficient and self-sufficient with the renowned 'Tottenham Pudding' pigswill and salvage drives. Locals recall making full use of their gardens for growing food and ensuring no scrap was ever wasted. Many local children were evacuated to safety and women once again operated the machinery of industry as Haringey dug-in for the duration.

The bombing of Haringey started in August 1940 and ended with the V2 rockets in 1945. In counting its dead, Haringey reflected on its relative good fortune since the devastation in other boroughs, particularly in London's East End, was far greater. Nevertheless the raids took their toll and many lives and homes were destroyed.

Haringey's experiences for each of the two wars were of course different but the spirit of its people remained very much the same. During both periods, people served their country proudly and with commitment despite the suffering and hardships. Their charitable nature was demonstrated through their work for fundraising schemes, when they made clothes for the comfort of the troops, and as they showed kindness to those displaced by the hostilities. The destruction of homes, the trials of rationing, relying on the help from complete strangers, the loss of loved ones in far off lands and also at home brought people together whatever their background. The rigid class and social barriers that had once previously divided people before the Second World War gradually began to erode.

The glimpses of life in Haringey seen in this collection of photographs captures some of the personal memories of a London borough at war. Some of these stories may already be familiar, others have never been revealed before, and yet others are still to be told.

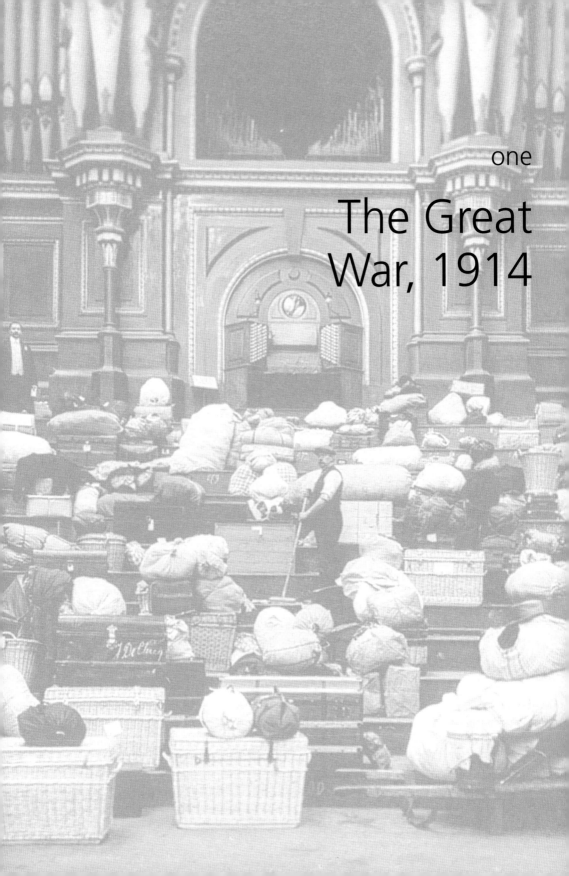

one

The Great War, 1914

Shops from 261-267 West Green Road in Tottenham with patriotic decorations to celebrate Queen Victoria's Diamond Jubilee in 1897. The late nineteenth to early twentieth century was an era of Empire building amongst the great power rivalries both within Europe and elsewhere. Britain had been involved with different conflicts in far-flung parts of the world and so for those living in Tottenham, Hornsey and Wood Green, war was not new.

The signs wish success to the Tottenham carnival which raised money for the local hospital and for wounded soldiers and sailors returning home, as well as 'Good Luck to the Irish' – an indication of the large numbers of Irish men living locally who were serving in the British army. Poverty and the need for an income, rather than warlike dispositions, would often have been the reason for these men to enlist.

Ambreville
Chez — Ferrier — en — Gatinais
Loiret, France
Thursday, 6 P.M

Dearest Mother,
            I received your nice letter last night and
was very pleased with it. I'm sorry I can't return
just now, but hope the war will soon be over.
Anyhow there is no need to worry for me here
in the centre of France, where we shall be
a long way from any fighting.
        - Also I'm very happy here. Every day
I go on my bicycle for a good ride. We are near
to Ferrier-en-Gatinais, where I go every day.
        - You would laugh if you saw
some of the courses for our meals.
Besides having 20 (no exaggeration) eggs
in an omelete, we had, yesterday, a
huge bowl of cream (big as your vegetable dish)
for one course. Made me think of Slexton's 3d
of cream.
        I expect you saw a difference in Una
when you filled and when I return she
will have grown quite a big girl.
        I'm getting on very well with my
French here and they (Especially, Mrs Carnijac)
help me in every way.

When war was declared in Europe on 4 August 1914, sixteen-year-old Sydney Smith was trapped in France on a school exchange trip. Syd wrote to his mother in St Alban's Crescent in Wood Green: 'I am sorry I can't return just now but hope the war will soon be over. Anyhow there is no need to worry for me here in the centre of France where we shall be a long way from any fighting'. By 14 August, Syd was back home. His only loss was his beloved new bicycle that had to be abandoned in France.

The cast of *The Magic Fan* from the High School for Girls and Kindergarten at 268 Wightman Road. They performed their grand evening concert on 25 March 1914 at the Allison Hall in Allison Road in Harringay. These young children were soon to witness 'the war to end all wars'. For them, growing up meant facing the reality of four long, terrible and uncertain years of war. Some were never to see their brothers, fathers or neighbours again.

Opposite above: A military camp in 1909. Frank Pulleyn (middle row, second right) of Turnpike Lane in Hornsey poses with comrades of the 9th Battalion of the London Regiment (Queen Victoria Rifles, Territorial Force). Frank and his brothers had gone to boarding school and on leaving, like fellow pupils, they joined the army part-time. The Territorial Force – 'Terriers' – was formed in 1908 following a reorganisation of the army's former militia and volunteer units. Terriers trained at weekends, in the evenings and sometimes at summer military camps.

Within the grounds of the Prince of Wales Hospital, the wounded soldiers relaxed playing cards in September 1914. The newspapers described the patients as 'very anxious to get back to the Front again'. Such stirring words must have helped with the appeal for volunteers to join the army. The early response was very enthusiastic amongst bands of youngsters who paraded in the local streets wearing paper hats, carrying wooden swords and singing patriotic songs.

14 the initial
d passed and the
lunteering to
ly. This Special
ued on 17 October
was displayed in the Orderly
. of Hornsey's Central Public
rary (then in Tottenham Lane).
:equested that men on National
.eserve of the Hornsey Battalion
Middlesex Division) formed a
>mpany for special guard duties,
nlisting for a year or the duration of
he war.

Opposite, above: Three days after war was
announced, troops were sent from the
British Expeditionary Force to France.
By 10 September 1914, the Prince of
Wales Hospital at Tottenham Green
had seen the arrival of some of the first
wounded soldiers. Here the walking
casualties are being assisted to the door.

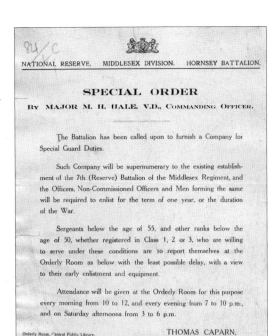

NATIONAL RESERVE.   MIDDLESEX DIVISION.   HORNSEY BATTALION.

SPECIAL ORDER
By MAJOR M. H. HALE, V.D., Commanding Officer.

The Battalion has been called upon to furnish a Company for Special Guard Duties.

Such Company will be supernumerary to the existing establishment of the 7th (Reserve) Battalion of the Middlesex Regiment, and the Officers, Non-Commissioned Officers and Men forming the same will be required to enlist for the term of one year, or the duration of the War.

Sergeants below the age of 55, and other ranks below the age of 50, whether registered in Class 1, 2 or 3, who are willing to serve under these conditions are to report themselves at the Orderly Room as below with the least possible delay, with a view to their early enlistment and equipment.

Attendance will be given at the Orderly Room for this purpose every morning from 10 to 12, and every evening from 7 to 10 p.m., and on Saturday afternoons from 3 to 6 p.m.

Orderly Room. Central Public Library,
Tottenham Lane, Hornsey, N.
17th October, 1914.

THOMAS CAPARN.
Organizing Officer and Acting Adjutant.

Lord Kitchener issued a call for volunteers to increase numbers of the regular army. Volunteers were assigned to units called New Armies. Men aged between nineteen and the new upper limit of forty-five years enlisted for the duration of the war. This postcard of 'Kitchener's Recruits' in Chatham was sent by new recruit Lew Wilkins to his family in Glenwood Road in Harringay. He writes: 'I am still in the land of the living. Kind regards to all at home.'

The west front of Mr. Wm. Smith's shop, 536, High-road, after the attack of Friday. Another window of similar size in the north front was also smashed.

William Smith's at 536 Tottenham High Road in 1915. Anti-German feelings heightened at particular moments. On 7 May 1915, the passenger liner *Lusitania* was sunk by a German torpedo off the coast of Ireland. This initiated a backlash of anti-German riots. One local recalls, 'The public of Tottenham got very angry and smashed their windows. One jeweller's was on the corner of Dowsett Road – it's still there today – he was a German and they smashed his shop before the police could get there. A few nights later they went and did the same to the bakers up the road.'

Mr. W. WERNST,

Butcher, 751, High Rd., Tottenham

wishes the Public to know that he will take immediate action against anyone saying or imputing that he is not English or not born in England.

In May 1915 about twenty shops suffered damage in Tottenham alone. Over 3,000 people had assembled in West Green Road. Many were women with large hats, forming screens from behind which rioters threw missiles. In response to the riots, some traders displayed notices saying 'All English firm' or 'No Germans served here'. Percy Alden MP wrote to newspapers regretting the persecution and supporting William Smith, the jeweller, highlighting that although Smith was born on German soil, he came to England as a baby and did not know the German language. It argued that he hadn't known he had to be naturalised and that his children were all English born.

Opposite, above: The police station in Tottenham High Road, *c.* 1914. Large numbers of Germans and Austrians had been living in Tottenham for years; at the outbreak of war, suspicion of espionage and hostility was shown towards them. As a protective caution, they registered their addresses and occupations with the police. Newspapers record cases against 'enemy aliens': 'Rudolf Schmidt, a German subject, charged with keeping on his premises four homing pigeons without a permit. The pigeons were produced in court. A detective said that, although not a pigeon expert, he thought these birds were capable of carrying messages. The prisoner said he only bred pigeons for eating.'

With the German invasion and occupation of Belgium, thousands of Belgian refugees arrived in Britain. From September 1914, Alexandra Palace was closed to the public and became a transit centre, providing temporary accommodation for the displaced refugees. The Belgians arrived at all hours of the day and sometimes in the middle of the night. They were disorientated, weak and tired. The grand Willis organ in the Great Hall was used as a baggage depot, storing what little belongings they had brought with them.

In response to appeals for clothing and boots for the Belgians, local people and kind American friends rallied round with collections. Volunteers manned the depots giving out the goods to new arrivals. With the large amount of clothing donated, the depots became known as 'Oxford Street'. Further appeals had to be made to stop any more 'top hats, mourning suits and large ladies' hats' from being delivered to the Palace as these were not at all suitable for the needs of the refugees.

Alexandra Palace was transformed for the refugees. The skating rink and badminton suite became dormitories and the Great Hall was used both for sleeping and feeding quarters. The warmest part of the building became the hospital. For refugees an average stay at the Palace was two or three days whilst arrangements were made for more permanent homes elsewhere in the country. Help was needed to cope with feeding the large numbers passing through and some of the Belgians – as seen here – assisted the Palace's catering staff.

Queen Mary visited Alexandra Palace to express the nation's sympathy with Belgium's distress. The Belgian Minister was there to thank her, surrounded by young Belgians calling out '*Vive la Reine! Vive la Reine!*'. In March 1915, after six months as a transit centre, Alexandra Palace closed its doors to the refugees. Over 200,000 Belgians had arrived in this country with 38,000 passing through the Palace. Ally Pally's racecourse resumed briefly for the public in April 1915 but the five one-day fixtures proved to be the last for several years.

Top: In May 1915, the newspapers reported: 'It has now been decided that Alexandra Palace will be used for the detention of interned German civilians – not, as expected, for German prisoners of war. The Palace is being practically emptied so that none of the exhibits and amusements which remained during the housing of the Belgian refugees will be left in their places. Members of the military guard have already arrived and barbed wire entanglements are completed. In a short time it is expected that there will be about 3,000 Germans interned at Alexandra Palace.'

Above: The German civilian internees remained at the Alexandra Palace for the duration of the war. The work allocated to them included tending allotments and poultry, making toys and repairing jewellery or clothes. Internees suffered great mental and physical hardship in the terrible tragedy of being separated from their wives and children and in being deprived of their freedom. They were also unable to carry out their trade or profession. Once the war ended many were deported with their British-born families to Germany as complete strangers and penniless; some had been in this country all their lives and could not even speak the German language.

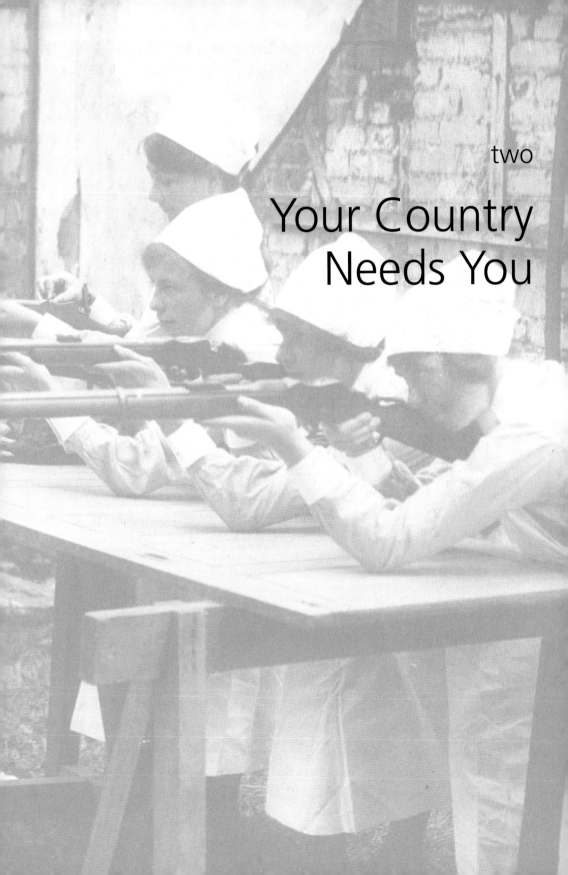

two

Your Country
Needs You

Signalling section of the 7th (Imperial Service) Battalion of the Middlesex Regiment in Gibraltar in 1914. Private F.C. Firth, a signaller in the Middlesex Regiment, recalls, 'Three of us decided to join up – you know the Kitchener poster "Your Country Needs You". We all wanted to be together. We decided to go to the recruiting office down the Tottenham High Road and the big, tall fellow was put on the Horse Guards, the middle one in the Artillery and I was put in the Infantry so we all got parted and we never saw one another again.'

Right: A National Registration card in 1915. Recruitment drives were not getting the large numbers of men needed for the military. The National Registration Act was introduced in July 1915; it allowed the government to find out how many men there were between the ages of fifteen and sixty-five and the types of work they did. Everyone had a card; this one was owned by Marion Dunn a machinist who lived at 3 Templeton Road in South Tottenham.

Opposite, above: Despite what so many had initially thought it became clear that the war would not be over by Christmas 1914. The short conflict envisaged by Lord Kitchener had already claimed 300,000 Frenchmen in the first five months alone. Christmas 1914 witnessed a brief, unofficial truce at the Western Front between the British and German soldiers. Rallying support and comfort for the troops, Princess Mary's Christmas Fund sent cards and tins with tobacco and cigarettes as gifts for every soldier.

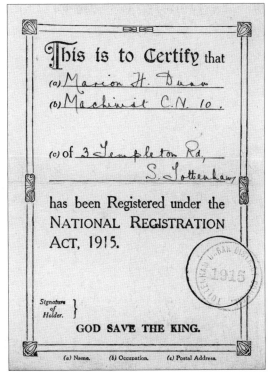

This is to Certify that
(a) Marion H. Dunn
(b) Machinist C.N. 10.

(c) of 3 Templeton Rd,
S. Tottenham

has been Registered under the NATIONAL REGISTRATION ACT, 1915.

Signature of Holder. }

GOD SAVE THE KING.

(a) Name.   (b) Occupation.   (c) Postal Address.

The 222nd Company Royal Engineers, No.1 Section, 33rd Division, pictured in June 1915 on Tottenham Marshes near the abrasives factory. All these men were recruited locally. The commanding officer is Lt E.L. Few MC (centre) one of the directors of English Abrasives. On his right is Sgt Minter and on his left is Cpl Morriss and Cpl Weir, all Spurs football players. Later in 1915, the government introduced the Derby Scheme for raising the numbers for the army even further. The results were still disappointing and so conscription was established in January 1916.

URGENT!!

To Men over Military Age, and under 18.

Amidst the roar during night raids, have you ever thought of what it is to stand or crouch in mud, slush and filth for weeks and months, amongst showers of bullets, shrapnel, splinters, poison gas and every abomination, as our boys at the Front have done? Death is busy all around them, while you are safe in dear old England.

Have you thought what our lot, and that of our women and children, would be, if our country were invaded by the Germans?

They come by air; what if they land on our coast? You can surely do **something.**

You are not of military age: join the Volunteer Force of your town.

Tottenham has a proud record; maintain this record in this latest effort.

Comradeship with your fellow townsmen will do you good; it will encourage them, and will assist the country in this hour of trial and danger.

Be prepared, be trained, become efficient, volunteer at once for **National Defence!**

PHILIP BUCK,

Chairman, Tottenham Council.

January 29th, 1918.

Crusha & Son, Printers, Tottenham and Wood Green.

Recruitment posters appeared throughout the war. This one, issued in January 1918 by Philip Buck the Chairman of Tottenham Council, appealed to men over the age of forty-one and under the age of eighteen to volunteer for National Defence at home. It did not mince its words: 'Amidst the roar during the night raids, have you ever thought of what it is to stand or crouch in mud, slush and filth for weeks and months amongst showers of bullets, shrapnel, poison gas and every abomination as our boys at the Front have done? Death is busy all around them while you are safe in dear old England.'

An overseas club certificate presented on Empire Day in 1916. The illustration demonstrates the unity of the allies of the British Empire throughout the world. Such certificates were usually issued to schoolchildren who raised money to help improve the comfort of the troops. Because of this fundraising, warm clothing and tobacco could be sent out to the Front on a regular basis. Such schemes also helped out families at home whose wage-earners were away in the forces.

Campaigners of the anti-war movement became more and more vocal in their opposition to a British conscript army. Locally the North London Herald League (NLHL) operated from 75 Grand Parade in Harringay moving in 1917 to 318 Green Lane.s The group arranged anti-war speakers for a network of organisations that met on Sundays in nearby Finsbury Park. Speakers included R.M. Fox, a pacifist, socialist, Quaker and chairman of the NLHL, as well as Sylvia Pankhurst of the Women's Movement.

The Friends' Meeting House at 594 Tottenham High Road. When conscription became law, some people identified themselves as conscientious objectors. Amongst these was Fred Murfin, a printer originally from Lincolnshire. Fred had attended Friends meetings in Tottenham but did not become a member. It was said that Quakers were to be exempt from military service and Fred did not want special treatment. A tribunal at Tottenham Town Hall sent Fred to battle in France with other objectors. They refused to fight and were court-martialled; their sentence was death by firing squad. By chance the British Minister of War was in France and, hearing of their fate, intervened. Their sentences were commuted to ten years' imprisonment.

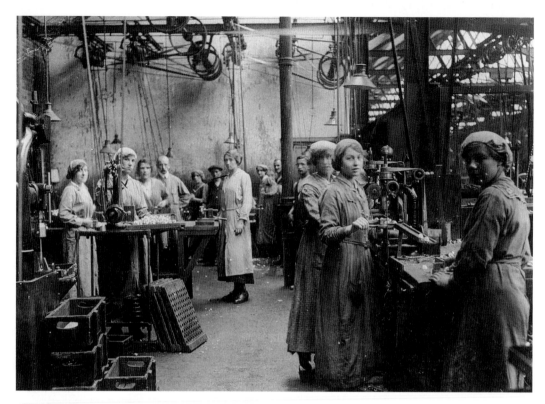

Above: Women munitions workers at the JAP factory in Northumberland Park, *c.* 1915. The labour shortage of 1915 led to the employment of women in industry. This was a grand departure from the pre-war position where women's work was largely in domestic service or, for married women, being a wife, mother and homemaker. Large factories in Tottenham turned their production-line to munitions, and these included the engineering firm of John A. Prestwich (JAP), Harris Lebus the furniture manufacturer and Gestetner's, the duplicating machine manufacturer. One woman had to do munitions work when her husband was wounded in the war: 'I went down to Gestetner's on munitions to earn a bit of money. We had a pound or guinea... and out of that guinea I had 6s rent to pay. So of course you can imagine it was hand-to-mouth. I couldn't do nursing because of having a young family. At Gestetner's I started at six o'clock in the morning and worked until six o'clock in the evening. I managed with the great help of my mother and a good neighbour.'

Opposite, above: Factory workers on Tottenham High Road, *c.* 1915. New opportunities saw one million women added to the British workforce between 1914 and 1918. One local comments, 'As time went by it became commonplace to see women taking on all kinds of jobs previously done by men – taking the fares on trams and buses and so on. Many smoked – a thing considered then as most unbecoming for a woman.' Women continued to make ends meet with homeworking. As one local said, 'In addition to taking in washing, my mother did fine crotchet work which she had to sell because we were so poor.'

Opposite, below: An unusual sight of nurses from the Prince of Wales Hospital in Tottenham Green being trained to fire a rifle as part of local defence. Having been issued with British-made Lee Enfield rifles, they are at target practice in the hospital grounds. Women's key contribution to the war effort boosted their demands for the vote; this was finally granted to those over the age of thirty at the end of the war.

Margaret Mitchell wears her husband Fred's trench coat and army cap. She worked as a booking office clerk at Finsbury Park station. On one occasion wounded soldiers were being transferred onto a train when a female porter caught sight of Margaret's brother Bill Pulfer on a stretcher and ran to tell her. Margaret was not allowed to see him. The family waited for a War Office letter which eventually arrived saying that Bill was in hospital in York. Working for the railway, Margaret got a pass – 'Oh he did look shocking! He recovered but was sent back to the Front. He had what was known as a clean wound.'

Opposite: To support men called up for service, the government encouraged women to join auxiliary military organisations as non-combatants. In 1917 the Women's Auxiliary Army Corps was formed with 57,000 women serving at home and overseas. Here Trissie Pulleyn of Turnpike Lane is pictured in around 1918 in WAAC uniform wearing a black armband; her husband Ted had been killed in action in November 1917 (see page 46). Seeing women in uniform and with shorter skirts (to save on material) caused a stir in social circles at first.

SAINT GEORGE'S - ENGLAND'S DAY.

DRUM-HEAD SERVICE

IN THE

PLEASURE GROUNDS, MIDDLE LANE,

HORNSEY, on

SUNDAY, APRIL 22nd, 1917

At 3 p.m.

If wet Service will be held in the Hornsey Parish Church (St. Mary's, High St.)

Detachments of the O.T.C., 5th V.B. Middlesex Regiment,
County of Middlesex Motor Volunteer Corps,
Metropolitan Special Constabulary (Y Division),
1st Cadet Battalion Middlesex Regiment,   V. A. D. Nurses,
St. John Ambulance Brigade, British Red Cross Society,
Voluntary Aid Organisations, Church Lads' Brigade, Boy Scouts,
etc., etc., are expected, and

THE MAYOR & CORPORATION

WILL ATTEND.

Collection in Aid of the Mayor of Hornsey's Local War Fund.

ENGLISH FLAG DAY

SATURDAY, APRIL 28th,

IN AID OF THE

MAYOR OF HORNSEY'S LOCAL WAR FUND.

Printed by "The Hornsey Journal," Ltd., 30, Crouch Hill, N.

A patriotic bill poster advertising two collections in a week as contributions to raising money for the Hornsey Local War Fund in 1917. This included a service to commemorate St George's Day, which involved different volunteer and auxiliary service organisations, followed by the English Flag Day a week later.

'Our Tank Bank Julian'. There were many fundraising events organised for different causes – some on behalf of soldiers at the Front or their families, others for refugees or others as campaigns to buy military equipment for the army. Flags were sold by children and women as part of the collecting. Money was raised to build this tank, *Julian*, which was paraded in Tottenham on 9 March 1918.

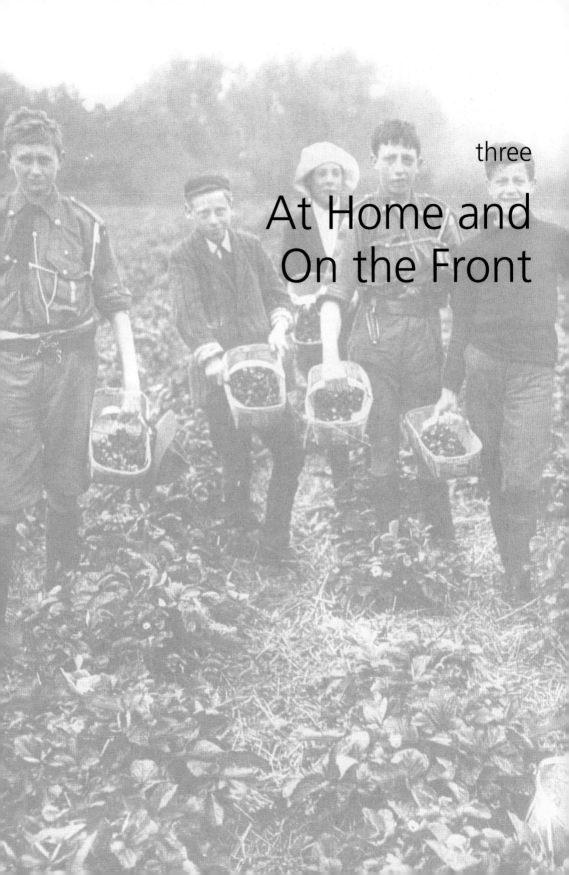

three

At Home and On the Front

The impact of the beginnings of war was soon seen on the streets in the locality. This scene shows the mounted cavalry of the King Edward's Horse Regiment passing through Bounds Green Road. In August 1914 this regiment was stationed at Alexandra Palace and Park where they started training troops to be mobilised in preparation for battle.

News from the Front came from either newspapers or wounded soldiers sent back home. Postcards, although censored by officers, were also sent. Many showed photographs of the troops as does this one posted by Lew Wilkins to his sister Edie of 77 Glenwood Road in Harringay. Sometimes official war films were screened. At the Canadian Rink Cinema in Tottenham, the words of David Lloyd George the Secretary of State for War read, 'Mothers, wives, sisters, your hearts will beat in honour and glory of the living and the dead. This graphic and stirring war film will bring the heroism, the tragedy and the glory of the battlefield before your eyes.'

Nothing could quite prepare soldiers for the harsh reality of the trenches. Here Pte Maffuniades (see page 45) stands equipped for battle with rifles, bayonets, binoculars and a periscope to see over the top. In an attempt to keep clean, troops had their hair cropped short, but conditions were so appalling that body lice could easily be picked up as could trench fever and epidemic typhus.

Amongst the horrors of the battlefield, beautiful silk-embroidered 'sweetheart cards' could be bought by troops from canteens and sent back home from the Front to loved ones. There were many different designs with flowers delicately entwined amongst the patriotic symbolism of flags and regimental colours.

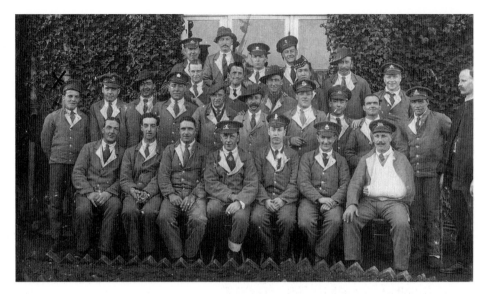

Syd Smith from Wood Green kept a diary of his experiences at the Front: '6 December 1917. Went down Sunken Road... and saw a whole body of Fritz's in our way. They soon cleared with a few bullets (I had five rounds left out of 120). Directly after this I felt as if someone had kicked me in the back. As I could feel a hole at back of my shoulder, I must be hit. I had to drop all my equipment. We kept on and I thought we should never get to Hindenburg Line where our people are.' Sent home from Cambrai, Syd (marked 'x', far left) recovered and convalesced in hospital.

Staff and wounded soldiers at North Middlesex Hospital; included in the image is Nurse Florence Lovett (in the back row, on the left) of Harold Road in South Tottenham. One local remembers, 'There were plenty of wounded soldiers about. They wore blue uniforms to show they were wounded. They'd got sticks and crutches, bandages and arms in slings... They always got well-treated – anybody who saw them would always give them a packet of fags. You didn't see them everyday – just now and again – and you got used to them.'

At the North Eastern Fever Hospital (now St Ann's Hospital) in St Ann's Road, Dr Ernest Goffe (centre) and his fellow medical colleagues treated many wounded soldiers sent back from the Front. Dr Goffe was originally from Jamaica and had been practicing medicine in London for over twenty years before the war started. With his wife, Dr Goffe moved to Kingston on Thames to practice as a GP after the war.

Edward George Cole was one of the proprietors of the long-established and family-run firm of Cole Potteries on White Hart Lane in Tottenham. Known as E.G. Cole, in 1899 he was elected to Tottenham Council, becoming chairman in 1917-1918. He was awarded an MBE for his service to the local military hospital during wartime. When he died on 22 June 1920, his obituary read: 'it would be difficult to find an area of public life in which he had not been involved.' His funeral was held with military honours.

Air raids brought the real dangers of warfare to the home front for the first time. The first air raid in Britain hit Great Yarmouth and King's Lynn on 19 January 1915. Air raids in London began on 31 May 1915. Here a Zeppelin flies over Holy Trinity church in Tottenham High Road. These giant airships had far-range bombing capabilities. Susceptible to poor weather, they were large targets for British pilots. Many recall the Zeppelin flying over Tottenham and shot down in flames at Cuffley in Hertfordshire in September 1916: 'It was 11.30 p.m. The heavens were pierced by powerful beams from searchlights. The throbbing noise of the engines were recognised. Gradually the fiery monster began to sink… with wild cheers from the crowds who had assembled.'

Above: Although the First World War saw far fewer air raids than the Second World War, understandably public alarm nevertheless ran high. Information on what to do was published in newspapers to reassure the public. Special Constables, seen here equipped on their Royal Enfield sidecar, gave air-raid warnings. For some locals, the danger was not considered as perilous as others anticipated: 'The air-raid warnings were done by a policeman on a bicycle. He would blow his whistle and shout "Take cover, take cover" – which most of us didn't do because what was there to take cover from?'

Opposite, below: German blockades and their submarine campaign stopped ships transporting food to the UK and this lead to food shortages. Prompted to produce more food as part of the war effort, allotments were introduced for the first time. Posters were issued to encourage people to take on allotments. Like many others the nurses from the Prince of Wales Hospital in Tottenham turned their hands to digging up the land surrounding the hospital. It is said that they produced 24 tons of potatoes that season.

Special Constables were signed up to give support to the police force. Many men had been recruited for the armed forces and so police numbers had suffered. In addition to giving air-raid warnings, they oversaw the provision of shelters and the regulation of lighting restrictions. Their guard duties included protecting potentially sensitive sites in the area from enemy sabotage. Here two Special Constables pose operating a mobile machine-gun for local defence. It is likely that they are demonstrating a prototype for this Royal Enfield sidecar; it is suitably equipped for defence with its vee-twin engine manufactured in the JAP works at Tottenham (see page 26).

Pupils from Hornsey County School in Mattison Road in Harringay went in groups to Cambridge for fruit-picking and experienced the pleasures and hardships of land workers. As Emily Burke, a member of staff, wrote: 'They found that, judging by one's aches and pains, fruit was picked with one's back as well as with one's fingers. Henceforth a pot of jam, once merely a toothsome delicacy, was a symbol of personal victory over physical weariness and an important weapon of modern warfare.'

In addition to fruit-picking, the school helped by providing homes for Belgian refugees. Pupils even made sandbags for use in the trenches. On Flag Days they raised money for special causes to help soldiers and their families. Schoolchildren also sent knitting to an old pupil who was serving in the Navy who then distributed it to the youngest boys on his ship. Tragically this naval officer's ship was torpedoed and he died with his shipmates.

The countryside of Devonshire Hill Lane just before war began. At this time the South family owned Devonshire Hill Farm, the surrounding fields and nearby River House. The family ran South's Potteries in White Hart Lane, making flowerpots for the Lea Valley's market-gardening industry. In wartime the business's horses, used for transporting pots, were requisitioned and sent to France. Their fields by the potteries were also taken over for growing potatoes. By the late 1920s and '30s, this rural scene was only a memory as the London County Council 'cottage' estates were built.

A view of the High Street in Highgate Village, *c.* 1918. As time went on food shortages increased, and this became more and more apparent in 1917. Food price lists were issued by local authorities to help stop profiteering by shopkeepers. If a shop was overstocked on a particular product, the authorities would commandeer these goods and redistribute them elsewhere. From the end of 1917, food rationing was gradually introduced for different foodstuffs, firstly sugar and then butchered meat

Above: The two postcards on this page were sent by Charles Bellchambers, the proprietor of Bell's fruit stores at 15 Palace Parade in Muswell Hill. Writing in 1918 to his young daughter Biddy in Eastbourne, he reassured her that her rabbits were well and asked what fruit she wanted. With the blockades of the German U-boats, little foreign fruit and vegetables could be traded. However the nearby market-gardeners and nurseries of Tottenham and the Lea Valley were able to provide a healthy supply of fruit and vegetables. For the first time tomato-growing was introduced locally and proved to be a great success.

Left: Abundant displays of fruit at Bell's stores show a sign for 'homemade jam'. Despite the food shortages, recipes in the newspapers advised readers how to make do with the food that was available. The advice was coupled with complaints from women to the newspapers about teachers who taught cookery classes for economy meals. As coal was rationed too, they argued that the cost of fuel outweighed any benefits from the money saved on ingredients.

Above: During 1917 workers in different occupations went on strike throughout the country, their grievances being issues of wages, exemption from military service and food shortages. Earlier in May 1915, however, striking tram workers in Wood Green met with little sympathy from the public; they criticised the men of military age and said they were merely 'loitering aimlessly about'.

Left: Loading up carts in Barratt's sweet factory in Mayes Road in Wood Green. As one of the most important and largest employers in the district during the war years, Barratt's maintained its sweet production line by engaging women to carry out work usually done by men. In April 1917 the firm advertised for 'four strong women' to be stokers. By September 1917 the factory was blighted by the food shortages and was forced to put its staff on half-time working on account of the short supply of sugar.

Above: Everyday life carried on throughout the war, with people still celebrating births and marriages in the best way they could. In 1915 the wedding of William Edward Gardner and Mabel Thorogood, of Gladstone Avenue, on the Noel Park estate in Wood Green.

Left: On 27 November 1915, William Thomas Camper Atkinson married Grace Elizabeth Bloomfield at All Hallows church in Tottenham. They pose here on their wedding day possibly in the grounds of nearby Bruce Castle. The couple lived at the Atkinson family home and shop at 13 Church Road where William Atkinson Snr's violins were displayed for sale.

four

People at War

Charles Fouracre Greenlees fought as 2nd-Lt of the 9th Battalion of the Queen's Regiment. He was killed in combat on 1 July 1916. He was only twenty-one years old. According to local historian W.J. Roe, Charles was the only son of the Greenlees family. To his memory and for all those who served in the war they erected the war memorial cross situated near the entrance to All Hallows church in Tottenham.

Left: Arthur Thomas Cheek was born at 164 Church Road in Tottenham. With two of his three brothers, he enlisted as a Private or 'Tommy' with the Queen's Regiment. Arthur never returned. He is buried at Ypres in Belgium.

Opposite, below: On 15 March 1916, Muffins was awarded the Distinguished Conduct Medal for bravery in saving his captain's life. He had found Captain Roberts badly wounded. Under a hail of gunfire, Muffins half-carried, half-dragged his comrade back towards British lines. Only three months later, Muffins himself was killed by a gunshot. He was twenty years old. A letter of condolence reads: 'Nearly 100 mourners were present. He was buried in the military cemetery on top of a beautiful hill by the side of other brave men of the 10th and some French comrades. For myself, I can only say that I have lost one of my best men.'

Ectos Maffuniades was born in Tottenham in 1896. His father, originally from Greece, ran a printing firm in Paxton Road. Ectos attended Tottenham Grammar School for boys from 1905 to 1909. He was affectionately known as 'Muffins'. Like his fellow pupils, Ectos joined the army in 1914, serving with the 10th Battalion Royal Fusiliers. Here Pte Maffuniades stands with his mother at the family home at 9 Bruce Grove.

"MUFFINS" SAVES HIS CAPTAIN'S LIFE.

The Pulleyn family lived at 96 Turnpike Lane in Hornsey from 1902. This family portrait was taken in the garden in 1907. From left to right in the back row are Ted, Sissie, her twin Arthur and Frank; in the front row are Edie, their father Edward, the youngest Rene, their mother Sarah and Hettie. All three sons went to war but only one survived.

Ted or Sgt Edward Henry Pulleyn was one of the 9th Battalion of the London Regiment (Queen Victoria Rifles, Territorial Force). His enlistment as a part-time 'Terrier' meant that, in the event of war, he could be called upon for full-time service. Once war began, he was one of the first men sent out to the Front as part of the British Expeditionary Forces. Ted sits here (second from the right) with his army colleagues.

For his 'gallantry, endurance and excellent service rendered' in the fight for Hill 60 of May 1915, Sgt Ted Pulleyn was awarded the Distinguished Conduct Medal. He became a 2nd-Lt but was killed in action at Cambrai on 25 November 1917. He was twenty-seven years old. There is no known grave.

Ted left a wife, Trissie, and a baby daughter, Babs. This portrait of mother and child was taken in October 1917, a month before Ted's death. Trissie joined the Auxiliary Corps (see page 28). As the years went by after the war, her contact with the rest of the Pulleyn family gradually ceased.

Frank Pulleyn was a tailor's clerk in 1914 and was considered the dandy of the family being always well-dressed and dapper. He was also a keen sportsman and especially liked football. Like his brother Ted, he was already in the Territorials of the 9th Battalion of the London Regiment (Queen Victoria Rifles). When war came, he became a Private attached to the 2/20th Battalion.

A portrait of Violet May Pulleyn, who was known to her family as Babs. Their baby, Francis Stanton Pulleyn, was born in August 1916. Tragically Babs died in childbirth, aged only twenty-one. She left Frank, a widower, serving in the army, with his baby son brought up by his mother Sarah.

Fighting for his country in the bad conditions of the trenches, Frank contracted tuberculosis. Sent back home, he died in a military hospital in Bermondsey in August 1918, aged twenty-six. Frank's mother Sarah continued to bring up her grandchild, becoming the child's legal guardian. The young Francis lived at the family home at 96 Turnpike Lane until his death in 1985.

Before the war Arthur Allen Pulleyn had gone to Somerset to learn farming. Joining up, he was a member of the same regiment as his brothers. Recommended by his superiors for expert horsemanship, these skills helped keep him from the Front line and he served in Egypt and Jerusalem. This portrait was taken in 1918, when he was twenty-four years old. Arthur survived the war unscathed but seldom spoke of his experiences. As farming was in a depressed state after the war, Arthur became a civil servant. Following a failed marriage, he married his second wife Edith Braby from Hornsey in 1930 and had two children.

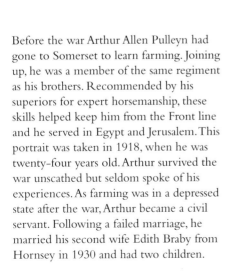

W.D.Tull.
Tottenham Hotspur.

Fighting for his country was not an easy undertaking for Walter Tull. The Manual of Military Law only allowed a limited number of Black men to become privates in the army. It also barred them from becoming commissioned officers. In 1916 Walter Tull was sent home with trench fever but, on recovery, attended officer training in Scotland. His superiors supported his desire to become an officer despite the regulations. Walter Tull became the first Black commissioned officer to serve in the British Army in this country. He was sent to the Italian Front in 1917 as a 2nd-Lt and was mentioned in dispatches for 'his gallantry and coolness'. Returning to France in 1918, he fought at the Second Battle of the Somme. The end of the war was only seven months away when Walter was killed on 25 March 1918 in no-man's land; his body was never recovered. The twenty-nine-year-old was described as 'brave and conscientious… The battalion and company have lost a faithful officer, and personally I have lost a friend.'

Opposite: Walter Tull played for Tottenham Hotspur football club from 1909 to 1912. His father, a joiner from Barbados, and his mother, from Folkestone, both died leaving Walter and his brother in an orphanage. Walter excelled at football, becoming one of Britain's first Black professional footballers. Whilst at Spurs, he experienced racial insults during a match against Bristol City. He left Spurs to join Northampton Town football club. Once war was declared, Walter signed up with friends from Spurs. Joining the Middlesex Regiment he fought with the 1st Football Battalion – one of the 'Pal' battalions. These battalions were formed of men who worked or socialised together and now served their country together. In all, thirteen Spurs players lost their lives in the war.

Thomas Turner, born in 1891, left school to become an electrician. His interest in aero engines made him join the Royal Flying Corps when war came. Due to his knowledge of engines, he became a corporal, instructing men on maintenance. Whilst working on a plane, the propeller spun round and shattered Thomas' left arm just above the elbow. He lost a lot of blood but survived the accident. After convalescence, he had to find another occupation as his previous work in the RFC was impossible for an amputee to do.

Above: The *Somerset Magazine*, Christmas Term 1917. For the very first time in its long history, Tottenham Grammar School for boys appointed female schoolteachers. Many of its schoolmasters had been called-up to fight. Once the war was over, the governors' wanted the school, in 1919, to return to its all-male environment. They thanked the women for their service and hoped they would find more suitable posts elsewhere. If any had found it difficult to find another position – or if the school had problems replacing them with male teachers – they said that the governors would consider re-engaging them but only on a temporary basis.

Opposite, below: Brother and sister, Alida and Louis Klemantski, relax in their garden at Brook House in Tottenham High Road, *c.* 1919. The home of this wealthy Jewish family was situated near the Edmonton border next-door to their family-run firm, the Boundary Wool & Hair Mills. In 1913, Alida met the poet Harold Monro. Sharing their love of poetry, Alida became an assistant at Monro's Poetry Bookshop in Bloomsbury. The war had put an end to the shop's publishing in 1916 but those who stayed at the shop until this time included the war poet Wilfred Owen. Alida and Monro married in 1920.

In 1913 the first eleven cricket team of Glendale County Grammar School in Wood Green lined up for this photograph. All these lads enlisted, including Syd Smith (first left in the middle row). One never returned – Eric Charles Braithwaite (in the centre of the middle row). The school magazine for December 1914 read: 'Sometimes in this quiet suburb, where beyond the darkened streets is the occasional glint of some distant searchlight and the more frequent presence of khaki-clad soldiers, there are few visible signs of the great conflict. We find it hard to realise that each day, while we carry on our work as usual, nations are being re-modelled.'

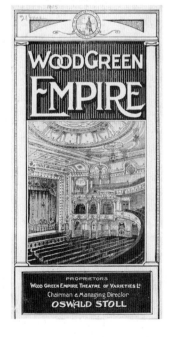

In May 1915, Sgt Maj. Harry Daniels, a recipient of the Victoria Cross, appeared at the Wood Green Empire. He received a rousing reception. He was honoured for his bravery at Neuve Chapelle on 12 March: 'I was instructed by my superior to go forward and cut the wire entanglements. What could I do? … Together we went forward, sometimes on our backs, and we began to cut the wire under heavy fire from the German machine guns. I stopped one – a bullet passed through my left thigh. Then I heard Tom make a noise, "What's up Tom?" A feeble reply came, "I've stopped it Dan – in my chest and stomach old man". Although mortally wounded, he pulled himself up and cut more wire, falling back exhausted. Again and again he did this until he sank to the ground and died. I saw a shell hole and crawled along. It was not big enough to cover me so I put my head down, which left my buttocks towards the enemy. "Have a go at that," I said to myself.' It was reported that the VC hero and his proud wife roared with laughter when he told this little incident.

five

Peace at Last

A handbill declaring the German's Armistice, which was implemented on the eleventh hour of the eleventh day in November 1918. This was only the first stage to the halt of four years' fighting – war finally ended with the Peace Treaty signed at Versailles in 1919. A resident said, 'I remember it plainly when the war ended. I was working and at eleven o'clock the maroon went up. I saw one of our workmates sitting there at a bench with her head in her hands crying her eyes out. Nobody had given it a thought – she had lost her husband in the war and there we all were, very happy, and she was heart-broken. That memory always stays in my mind.'

The German People Offers Peace.

The new German democratic government has this programme:

"The will of the people is the highest law."

The German people wants quietly to end the slaughter.

The German popular government therefore has offered an

Armistice

and has declared itself ready for

Peace

on the basis of justice and reconciliation of nations.

It is the will of the German people that it should live in peace with all peoples, honestly and loyally.

What has the new German popular government done so far to put into practice the will of the people and to prove its good and upright intentions?

a) The new German government has appealed to President Wilson to bring about peace.

It has recognized and accepted all the principles which President Wilson proclaimed as a basis for a general lasting peace of justice among the nations.

b) The new German government has solemnly declared its readiness to evacuate Belgium and to restore it.

c) The new German government is ready to come to an honest understanding with France about **Alsace-Lorraine.**

d) The new German government has restricted the **U-boat War.**

No passengers steamers not carrying troops or war material will be attacked in future.

e) The new German government has declared that it will withdraw all German troops back over the German frontier.

f) — The new German government has asked the Allied Governments to name commissioners to agree upon the practical measures of the evacuation of Belgium and France.

These are the deeds of the new German popular government. Can these be called mere words, or bluff, or propaganda?

Who is to blame, if an armistice is not called now?

Who is to blame if daily thousands of brave soldiers needlessly have to shed their blood and die?

Who is to blame, if the hitherto undestroyed towns and villages of France and Belgium sink in ashes?

Who is to blame, if hundreds of thousands of unhappy women and children are driven from their homes to hunger and freeze?

The German people offers its hand for peace.

The premises of S. Holland, the cycle dealers, at 6 Queens Parade in Hornsey. Peace was celebrated with lavish festooning of shops: 'Streets became gay with flags and khaki-clad lads and lasses were seen arm in arm in rows, dancing and giving vent to feelings of joy in every conceivable manner. Many assembled at the few public houses that were open and drank all sorts of toasts that commended themselves to their pent-up feelings. In the evening, thousands took to the streets and participated in street-play to the accompaniment of mouth-organs, squeakers or anything that made a noise – the more hideous the better.'

A portrait of the Ward fa,ily at the Armistace in 1919. The six Ward brothers returned home from war to their mother and their families. They went back to the family business running Ward Stores, a large department store selling furniture, furnishings and jewellery, on the corner of Seven Sisters Road and Tottenham High Road. A local landmark, the business ran successfully for another fifty years.

Street parties were organised to celebrate Peace Day in July 1919. This one in Clyde Road in Tottenham brought everyone together. The men dressed up in their old uniforms, some sporting German helmets that they had brought back from the Front as souvenirs. The children were given cups and saucers to commemorate the day.

Opposite, above: A Peace Day street party at Steele Road in Tottenham in July 1919. Some celebrated their parties with children dressing up in costumes. Alongside the Union Jack the flag of the 'American Stars and Stripes' was flown acknowledging the USA's role in the war from April 1917. Some locals had memories of American servicemen at St Ann's Hospital: 'The Yanks would come out of the ward and get on the fence and as we came down the road, they'd say "Here son, go get us a bottle of beer." Give us a tanner for going – they didn't know the money.'

As part of the peace celebrations at school some teachers instructed their pupils to bring in cakes and food. They made lemonade and had a feast. In all the Tottenham schools the council gave the children a commemorative victory medal made of lead. On one side was an image of Tottenham town hall and on the reverse was the figure of winged victory. It was inscribed 'Victorious Allies 1918'. This medal was given to G.F. Bloomfield who attended Belmont Road School.

In Wood Green all the schools were invited to participate in a dramatic Peace Pageant held in July 1919 at Wood Green Recreation Ground. All the children were in costume celebrating the history of Wood Green. Included in this historical line-up was the rebellion of Boudicca against the Romans as she passed through Wood Green from St Alban's to London; the visit of Queen Elizabeth I in 1590; the opening of the New River in 1618 (seen here) and Wood Green's independence from Tottenham in 1894.

This photograph shows Bounds Green School's tableau of the Elizabethan period for the Wood Green School's Peace Pageant. A seven-year-old Constance Gamage sits in the front row (second from the left). She said, 'This was just a part of it – I clearly remember a wonderful Queen Elizabeth with courtiers.'

Table 2

☞ IF FOUND, please drop this Certificate in a Post Office letter box.   Army Form Z. 11.

NOTICE.—"This document is Government property. It is no security whatever for debt, and any Person being in possession of it, either as a pledge or security for debt, or without lawful authority or excuse, is liable under Section 156 (9) of the Army Act to a fine of twenty pounds (£20) or imprisonment for six months, or to both fine and imprisonment."

PROTECTION CERTIFICATE AND CERTIFICATE OF IDENTITY
(SOLDIER NOT REMAINING WITH THE COLOURS).

Dispersal Unit Stamp and date of dispersal

Surname _SMITH_
(Block letters)

Dispersal Unit,

Christian Names _SYDNEY WALTER SCOTT_

= 9 APR 1919

CRYSTAL PALACE.

Regtl. No. _21278_   Rank _Pte_   Record Office _W.O. (Table 2)_

Unit _Blackheath_   Regt. or Corps _A.P.C._   Pay Office _Upper Thames St_

I have received an advance of £2.   † Address for Pay _66 St Albans Crescent_

(Signature of Soldier) _SS Smith_   _Wood Green N22_

The above-named soldier is granted 28 days' furlough from the date stamped hereon pending* __1__ (as far as can be ascertained) which will date from the last day of furlough after which date uniform will not be worn except upon occasions authorized by Army Orders.

* If for Final Demobilization insert 1.
  Disembodiment insert 2.
  Transfer to Reserve insert 3.

Theatre of War or } _4_
Command }

Born in the Year _1898_

Medical Category _BII Grade III_

Place of rejoining in } _Hounslow_
case of emergency }

Specialist Military }
Qualification }

† As this is the address to which pay and discharge documents will be sent unless further notification is received, any change of address must be reported at once to the Record Office and the Pay Office as noted above, otherwise delay in settlement will occur.

R. Wade

This Certificate must be produced when applying for an Unemployed Sailor's and Soldier's Donation Policy or, if demanded, whenever applying for Unemployment benefit.

Date____ = 9 APR 1919 Office of Issue_____ Policy issued No. _A22 059115_

This Certificate must be produced when cashing Postal Drafts and Army Money Orders for weekly pay whilst on furlough.

The Postmaster will stamp a ring for each payment made.   P.O. Stamp to be impressed here when Savings Bank Book is issued.

(1)

Once war was over, reintroducing former troops into civilian life was not easy for the government. Various unpopular schemes were drawn up but in January 1919 a more equitable demobilisation scheme was introduced. Age, length of service and how many times a man had been wounded were considered. Generally those that had served longest in the forces were demobilised first. Syd Smith had been wounded and was demobilised in April 1919. He was issued with these identity papers.

This out-of-work donation book was issued to all demobilised troops. Promised a land 'fit for heroes' by Lloyd George, some war veterans and their families endured hardship and unemployment on their return home. For those women and older men who had kept industry going during the war years, they too often experienced unemployment once ex-servicemen returned to replace them.

Above: Thomas Turner (in the centre) lost his left arm whilst carrying out his duties in the Royal Flying Corps (see page 52). Thomas nonetheless continued to pursue his sports – even cycling on a tandem bicycle as seen here outside Roehampton Hospital. Thomas could no longer follow his trade as an electrician and so retrained in the art of heraldry and became a skilled coach-liner. Thomas settled down with his family in Bruce Grove, Tottenham.

Opposite, below: Members of Wood Green Council's Education Committee and Day Nursery Committee gather with visitors for the opening ceremony of the Stuart Villas Centre in Stuart Crescent on 6 July 1918. During the First World War it helped young mothers who had to work by providing nursery places for their children. These women were either war widows or their husbands had been severely wounded in the war. As one woman remembers, 'I didn't decide to become a mid-wife until Pop came home from the war. I went in to take my diplomas – it wasn't too easy and you had to pay for it. You had to find a lump sum of £50. Pop wasn't working – he was a semi-invalid. It was with the help of my mother with the expenses that I got through really. And Dr Gaston – he put down £20 towards my fee.'

Horrified with how her wounded brother, Bill, had been treated, Margaret Mitchell was determined '… never, ever, to sanction war again. I saw men without legs. Men without arms. In wheelchairs. Our Bill – when he applied for a pension, they told him that they had saved the arm and he was not entitled. If they amputated the arm it would have been different.' Margaret's husband, Fred, died in 1926 as a reult of his war wounds. During the economic slump of the 1920s, Margaret sought to better the conditions for the poor and working-classes and became a founder of the Tottenham National Unemployed Workers Movement. This picture shows Margaret and a Welsh miner walking down Tottenham High Road.

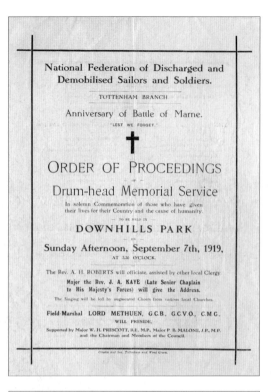

National Federation of Discharged and
Demobilised Sailors and Soldiers.

TOTTENHAM BRANCH

Anniversary of Battle of Marne.
"LEST WE FORGET."

✝

ORDER OF PROCEEDINGS
OF
Drum-head Memorial Service

In solemn Commemoration of those who have given
their lives for their Country and the cause of humanity.

— TO BE HELD IN —

DOWNHILLS PARK
— ON —
Sunday Afternoon, September 7th, 1919,
AT 3.30 O'CLOCK.

The Rev. A. H. ROBERTS will officiate, assisted by other local Clergy

Major the Rev. J. A. KAYE (Late Senior Chaplain
to His Majesty's Forces) will give the Address.

The Singing will be led by augmented Choirs from various local Churches.

Field-Marshal LORD METHUEN, G.C.B., G.C.V.O., C.M.G.,
WILL PRESIDE.

Supported by Major W. H. PRESCOTT, R.E. M.P., Major P. B. MALONE, J.P., M.P.
and the Chairman and Members of the Council.

Crusha and Son, Tottenham and Wood Green.

The Order of Proceedings of a Drum-head
service was held on 7 September 1919
at Downhills Park to commemorate the
fifth anniversary of the Battle of Marne.
From 7-10 September 1914 the morale of
British and French troops soared as they had
succeeded in forcing the Germans to retreat
at the Battle of Marne. The total of British
casualties amounted to 1,701 of all ranks
– either killed, wounded or missing.

In 1919, eight-year-old Amy Green sent this
picture of herself on this patriotic postcard
to her grandmother living in Hackney.
The Green family lived in Vartry Road in
South Tottenham. Her father Edwin had
been a sergeant in the regular army before
the war, spending many years in India, and
was working as a tram driver when war
broke out. He was recalled to the army and
sent to train recruits for the Royal Field
Artillery. Her mother, also Amy, worked in a
munitions factory as well as looking after her
young family.

Over 40,000 people attended the unveiling ceremony of the Tottenham War Memorial at Tottenham Green on Sunday 17 June 1923. The sculpture of Winged Peace was unveiled by HRH Princess Louise, the Duchess of Argyll, as she held the hand of a young boy, the son of a fallen Tottenham soldier. The memorial was dedicated by the Bishop of Willesden and is inscribed, 'Erected by the inhabitants of Tottenham in proud and grateful memory of her sons who fell in the Great War, 1914-1918. Greater love hath no man than this. Pass not without Remembrance. Their Name Liveth Forevermore'. For both sides of the conflict, over 9.4 million lives were lost. Of this number 5.4 million were Allied troops. For Britain, there were over 3 million casualties in warfare, with 658,700 dead. Millions more lived on with disabilities, both physical and mental.

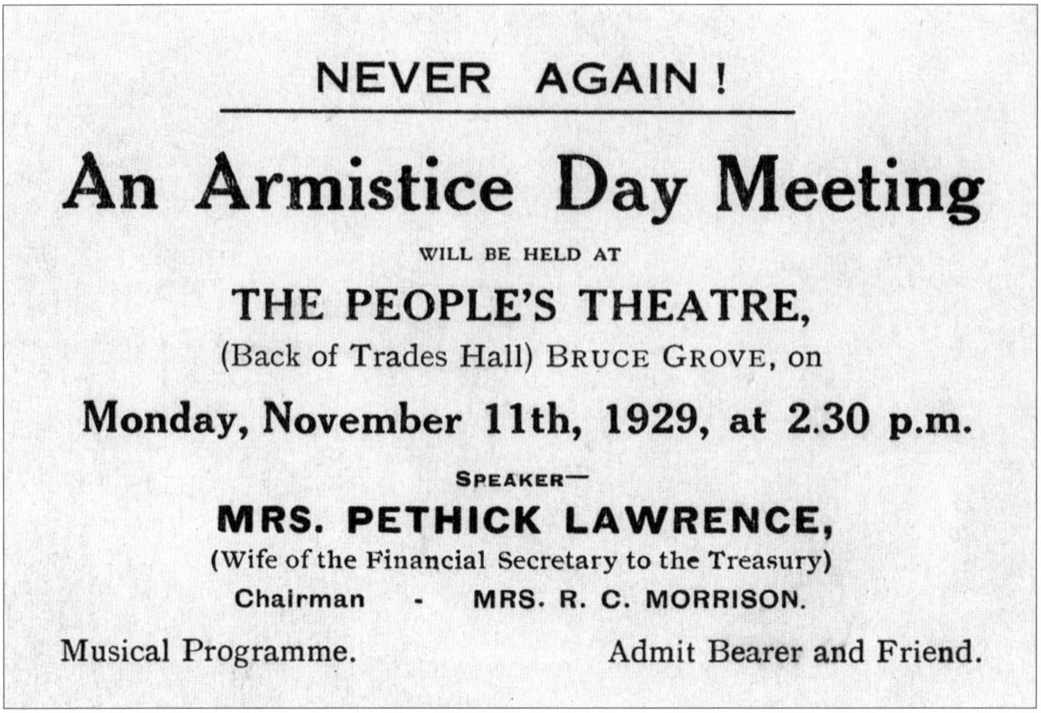

NEVER AGAIN!

An Armistice Day Meeting

WILL BE HELD AT

THE PEOPLE'S THEATRE,

(Back of Trades Hall) BRUCE GROVE, on

Monday, November 11th, 1929, at 2.30 p.m.

SPEAKER—

MRS. PETHICK LAWRENCE,

(Wife of the Financial Secretary to the Treasury)

Chairman - MRS. R. C. MORRISON.

Musical Programme.   Admit Bearer and Friend.

An invitation to an Armistice Day meeting on 11 November 1929. Ten years after the end of the First World War, events were held on Armistice Day throughout the boroughs of Tottenham, Hornsey and Wood Green to push for a peaceful future. Another ten years later, the hope for peace was dashed with the outbreak of the Second World War in 1939.

six

Britain
Prepares for
War

Below the advertising hoardings in a side street of South Tottenham, anti-fascist graffiti urges people to oppose the threat posed by the Blackshirts led by Sir Oswald Mosley. The years of economic depression in the early 1930s and the ensuing discontent had given Mosley and his followers opportunity to stir up feelings against the Jews. Many people from Haringey joined those from the neighbouring borough of Hackney to actively demonstrate against Mosley's campaign of violence and intimidation. Margaret Mitchell recalls, 'We from Tottenham had a very good contingent fighting the Blackshirts... it was time they put a stop to it and that was that.'

A Hornsey Civil Defence contingent on parade outside Hornsey town hall on 3 September 1939 prior to the main parade in Hyde Park. They were awaiting the announcement from Prime Minister Neville Chamberlain of Britain's declaration of war. Until 1943 all Civil Defence personnel served on a voluntary basis with the majority of its ranks in full-time employment.

Opposite, below: Anderson air-raid shelters being unloaded onto a horse-drawn railway cart at South Tottenham station goods yard in April 1939. Tottenham led the country in being the first borough to distribute Anderson shelters on a large scale and so acted as a trial ground for the Home Office. A local resident recalls, 'The shelter was half-buried in the ground with earth on top…Water would seep in… When the raids were on we'd go down at about eight or ten o'clock at night and come up at about seven or eight o'clock in the morning.'

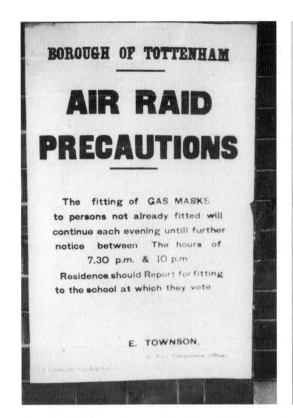

BOROUGH OF TOTTENHAM

AIR RAID
PRECAUTIONS

The fitting of GAS MASKS
to persons not already fitted will
continue each evening until further
notice between The hours of
7.30 p.m. & 10 p.m.
Residence should Report for fitting
to the school at which they vote

E. TOWNSON,

BOROUGH OF TOTTENHAM

A.R.P. BLACK-OUT
AUGUST 9TH - 10TH
Lights to be Extinguished or Screened.

IMPORTANT NOTICE

Between the hours of 12.30 and 4 a.m. in the early morning of Thursday, 10th August, 1939, all

(a) Owners of illuminated signs, advertisements and all shop windows,
(b) Garages and commercial premises open all night,
(c) Factories and workshops engaged on night work,
(d) Hotel and shop proprietors,
(e) Occupiers of private premises,

are asked to extinguish all external lights, and to screen or extinguish all internal lighting.

All street lighting will be restricted and vehicles should, so far as possible, keep off the roads during these hours, but no lights or power appliances will be cut off from the mains.

This Exercise is an essential step in securing the Safety of London from Air Attack—but it can only be successful with the co-operation of the Public.

NOTE.—If owing to weather conditions it is necessary to postpone the Black-out to the following night, an announcement will be Broadcast in the 6 p.m. News on the 9th August.

YOUR LOCAL A.R.P. SCHEME STILL REQUIRES approximately 2,000 VOLUNTEERS for the following Services:

CASUALTY SERVICES.—Women over 18. Men over 30. Ambulance Drivers, Nurses and Stretcher Bearers.
DECONTAMINATION.—Men over 25.
RESCUE, SHORING & DEMOLITION.—Men over 25. Experienced Demolishers, Builders and Carpenters.
WARDENS.—Women over 25. Men over 30.

Apply to—Local A.R.P. Office, 4 Norma Villas, N.15

C. F. Wilkinson (T.U.), Printer, 64 Lordship Lane, N.17

Above, left: With the horror of First World War gas attacks on the battlefield very much in living memory, an information poster directs public attention to the fitting of gas masks as part of Air-Raid Precautions. The misspelling of the word 'residents' suggests the poster was produced in a hurry. Though stories varied, parents encouragingly reported that the coloured gas masks for their children were an ideal toy: 'they think they are like a comic mask and wear them all day.'

Above, right: Notification of an Air-Raid Precaution Blackout exercise in August 1939. Although the first Air-Raid Precautions Act came into effect in 1937 active preparations had begun in Haringey much earlier and comprehensive schemes were quickly approved. Wood Green Magistrates initially found themselves dealing with a number of cases of rowdy behaviour as young people took advantage of the cover of almost total darkness. Before restrictions were modified, defying the very purpose of the Blackout by shining a torch to look for his £1 note cost one local man a fine of double the amount.

Opposite: A price list displayed in February 1938 at Laceys grocer's shop in Tottenham High Road indicates a variety of food products freely available before the outbreak of hostilities. The first ration books were issued in 1940. This measure was taken initially to prevent more wealthy people from stockpiling food and to ensure a fair distribution. Over time an adult ration for one week was reduced to 8oz fat (of which only 2oz could be taken as butter), 2oz tea, 8oz sugar, 1oz cheese and 4oz bacon or ham. Meat was rationed by price as opposed to weight and included bone, fat and gristle. Bread was not rationed until after the war – it came as a bit of a shock when it was rationed in 1946.

February, 1938
463 High Road,
TOTTENHAM

LACEYS

3 Grand Parade,
HARRINGAY
(3 doors from The Salisbury)

Grocers and Provision Merchants

SUGAR

Granulated TATE & LYLE	... 2 lb. Nett	$4\frac{1}{2}$d
Lump TATE & LYLE	... 2 lb. Nett	$5\frac{1}{2}$d
Preserving TATE & LYLE	4 lb. Bag 10d	12 lb. 2/5

Breakfast Foods

Shredded Wheat ...		
Plasmon Oats ...	Pkt.	6^{1}_{2}d
Rice Crispies ...		
All Bran		
Puffed Wheat or Rice ...		6d
Weetabix ...	$5\frac{1}{2}$d	$8\frac{1}{2}$d
Scotts Porage Oats ...5d		$8\frac{1}{2}$d
Quaker Oats ...	$3\frac{1}{2}$d	$7\frac{1}{2}$d
Kellog's Corn Flakes ...		
Post Toasties ...		4^{1}_{2}d
Quaker Corn Flakes ...		
Force ...		5d
Fry's Cocoa, Loose ... lb		$7\frac{1}{2}$d

CEREALS

Rolled Oats QUICK COOKING	2 lb.	$4\frac{1}{2}$d
Tapioca ...	lb.	$3\frac{1}{2}$d
Rice, Finest Carolina	lb.	4d
Rice, Finest Empire	lb.	3d
Butter Beans (new crop) ...	lb.	3d
Pearl Barley ...	lb.	2d
Split Peas ...	lb.	3d
Haricots ...	lb.	2d
Robinson's Groats or Barley		
$\frac{1}{3}$'s $\frac{1}{2}$'s lbs.	$3\frac{1}{2}$d $6\frac{1}{2}$d	1/1

JAMS

PURITAN BRAND—

Strawberry 2s Whole Fruit		8d
Raspberry ...		
Black Currant ...		
Apricot ...		8^{1}_{2}d
Damson ...		
Plum Stoneless ...		6d
Marmalade Orange ...		7d

HARTLEY'S—

Strawberry	1 lb. $9\frac{1}{2}$d 2 lb.	1/5$\frac{1}{2}$
Black Currant	1 lb. 9d 2 lb.	1/5
Raspberry		
Apricot ...	lb. $8\frac{1}{2}$d 2 lb.	1/3$\frac{1}{2}$
Plum Stoneless	lb $7\frac{1}{2}$d 2 lb	1/1$\frac{1}{2}$

ROBERTSON'S—

Golden Shred OR SilverShred	1s 7d	2s 1/-
Bramble Jelly	lb. 7d 2 lb.	1/0$\frac{1}{2}$
Ginger Marmalade	lb. $8\frac{1}{2}$d 2 lb.	1/3$\frac{1}{2}$

FLOUR

McDougall's PLAIN OR SELF-RAISING	3 lb.	9d
Lacey's Self-Raising	3 lb.	6d

BUTTER COUNTER

Lard Pure	- lb	$6\frac{1}{2}$d
Cheese Finest New Zealand	lb	$7\frac{1}{2}$d
Kraft Cheese	lb	1/-
Rindless Cheese	lb	8d
Butter Dutch Creamery Unsalted	lb	1/1
Butter Finest N Zealand Slightly Salt	lb	1/-
Margarine British Made	lb	4d
Trex OR Spry	½ lb. box 4d	lb. box $7\frac{1}{2}$d

BACON COUNTER

Back Finest Breakfast	- -	1/-
Finest Streaky		8d
Finest Collar Rashers		1/-
Dripping Pure Beef	-	6d

Canned Fruits

Oranges LARGE TINS ...		$3\frac{1}{2}$d Tin
Pineapple LARGE TINS		2 for $6\frac{1}{2}$d
Plums Large Tins		$4\frac{1}{2}$d
Peaches Large Tins Sliced		$7\frac{1}{2}$d
Pears, Bartlett Large Tins		8d
Pineapple Giant Size		$4\frac{1}{2}$d
Loganberries Large Tins ...		$6\frac{1}{2}$d

CUSTARDS

Fulcreem	lb. Pkt.	$4\frac{1}{2}$d
Pearce Duff ...	12 Pts.	4d
Birds 5 pt. Pkt. 6d 10 pt. $9\frac{1}{2}$d Tins		1/2
Bestoval ...	12 pts.	$3\frac{1}{2}$d
Monk and Glass ½ lb. $4\frac{1}{2}$d 1 lb.		$7\frac{1}{2}$d

HEINZ GOODS

Beans—		
Small Size	$2\frac{1}{2}$d, 2 tins	$4\frac{1}{2}$d
Med. „	3d, 2 „	$5\frac{1}{2}$d
Large „ ...		4d
Tomato Ketchup	5d 7d	$10\frac{1}{2}$d
Spaghetti in Tomato	$3\frac{1}{2}$d	6d
Soups all kinds	$4\frac{1}{2}$d 6d	$11\frac{1}{2}$d

CHEF GOODS

Soups All kinds $3\frac{1}{2}$d tins, 2 tins		$6\frac{1}{2}$d
Tomato Ketchup ...		$4\frac{1}{2}$d
Peterkin Peas ...	lb tin	3d

Polishes, Soaps, etc.

Bluebell	... $7\frac{1}{2}$d size	5^{1}_{2}d
Brasso		
Mansion Floor Polish $4\frac{1}{4}$d $7\frac{1}{2}$d		1/2
Cobra Polish ...	$6\frac{1}{2}$d	1/1$\frac{1}{2}$d
Cherry Blossom 2d tin	2 for	$3\frac{1}{2}$d
	Med. $3\frac{1}{2}$d	Large $5\frac{1}{2}$d
Zebo Liquid Grate Polish $3\frac{1}{2}$d	$5\frac{1}{2}$d	$7\frac{1}{2}$d
Harpic ...	$5\frac{1}{2}$d $10\frac{1}{2}$d	1/3$\frac{1}{2}$d
Soap Flakes, Best ...	lb	$3\frac{1}{2}$d
Starch, quality ...	lb	$2\frac{1}{2}$d
Johnson's Wax $4\frac{1}{2}$d $8\frac{1}{2}$d		1/2$\frac{1}{2}$d
Candles 12ss 3d lb, 3lb Pkt.		8d
Rinso ...	3d $5\frac{1}{2}$d	$8\frac{1}{2}$d
Persil ...	3d	$5\frac{1}{2}$d
Oxydol ...	3d $5\frac{1}{2}$d	$10\frac{1}{2}$d
Fairy Soap ...		
Pear's Unscented		4d
Lifebuoy Toilet ...		
Lux „ ...		2^{1}_{2}d
Palmolive ...		

COFFEE

Camp 5d 8d 1/3d ("Cafe")		3/2$\frac{1}{2}$d
Lyons 5d $7\frac{1}{2}$d 1/- ("Cafe")		3/4$\frac{1}{2}$d
Distil ...	5d 7d	1/0$\frac{1}{2}$d
Lyon's French ...	$4\frac{1}{2}$d qr. tin	

SUNDRIES

Ryvita	8^{1}_{2}d	1/3$^{1}_{2}$d
Vita Wheat ...		
Farley's Rusks...	... 3d	$8\frac{1}{2}$d
Viota Tea Cakes ...		6d
Simco Cake Flour 4d each 2 pkts		$7\frac{1}{2}$d
Green's Sponge ...		5d
Bisto 2d $5\frac{1}{2}$d tins $8\frac{1}{2}$d		1/2$\frac{1}{2}$d
Marmite 5d $8\frac{1}{2}$d 1/2$\frac{1}{2}$d 2/1$\frac{1}{4}$d		3/9$\frac{1}{2}$d
Symington's Soups		
E.D.S. „	2	3^{1}_{2}d
Maggi's „ pkts.		
Colman's Mustard qr. tin		$7\frac{1}{2}$d
Lyle's Syrup ...	2 lbs.	$7\frac{1}{2}$d
Martineau Syrup	2 lbs.	$6\frac{1}{2}$d
Daddies Sauce ...	5d $7\frac{1}{2}$d	$11\frac{1}{2}$d
O.K. ...	4d $5\frac{1}{2}$d $7\frac{1}{2}$d	9d
Goat Milk $2\frac{1}{2}$d $3\frac{1}{4}$d large tin		4d
Del Monte Pilchards ...		$5\frac{1}{2}$d
Pastes Fish or Meat	Large Jars	$2\frac{1}{2}$d
Suet Shredded ½ lb. 5d lb. packet		$9\frac{1}{2}$d
Galloway's Cough Mixture		
$5\frac{1}{2}$d $9\frac{1}{2}$d		1/2$\frac{1}{2}$d
Sultanas Californian Golden		lb 6d
Raisins, seedless Californian ...		lb $4\frac{1}{2}$d
Currants (Greek) ...		lb 5d
Prunes Large Californian ...		lb 5d

KEEP THIS PRICE LIST FOR FUTURE REFERENCE

These prices are not special prices, but an indication of Laceys value for money.

In accordance with our usual practice, we make no extra charge for relief ticket customers who are given every consideration.

Infants at St Paul's School in Park Lane in Tottenham enjoy their free school milk in July 1939. When war was declared many children were evacuated from towns and cities for fear of imminent bombing raids. As this danger did not materialise for almost a year some parents thought it safe to bring their children home. This was a course of action they were soon to regret.

Opposite, below: Miss Wallace and Senior Librarian-to-be, Winnie Evans, of Tottenham Public library at Blunham Agricultural Camp near Bedford in August 1943. The notice between them highlights the Dig for Victory campaign. Such was the commitment to maximising output that by 1945 the country was importing only one third of its food requirement. This was due not only to a concerted effort on the part of the farms but also the efficient use of gardens and allotments. Remembering her family's air-raid shelter, a Tottenham resident tells of growing vegetables: 'We got all our salad and tomatoes, all along the top... lovely radishes, lettuces...'

Right: A ration book for clothing issued to D.E. Williams of Glenwood Road in Harringay. Clothes were forever being altered and refashioned to fit another member of the family. No cloth was wasted and a cartoon of the day was scarcely exaggerating when it depicted a tailor being asked to turn a woman's skirt back into her husband's dinner jacket. 'Make do and mend' was the order of the day.

A local waste deposit for paper, tins and bottles, referred to as salvage bags. The essential task of recycling household waste was continually emphasised and regularly promoted. The message that nothing must be wasted and everything can be reused was instilled into the nation's collective conscience.

A deposit for waste food outside the gas company's building in The Broadway in Hornsey. As directed on the sign people could alternatively hand their waste food to the dustmen. The contents of these 'swill bins' would be collected regularly and taken to the salvage works for processing. The 'Do Not Waste Food' campaign meant literally every scrap.

Queen Mary, the mother of King George VI, inspects the crude material of 'Tottenham Pudding', on the occasion of her visit to the Tottenham Borough Refuse Disposal and Salvage Works at Down Lane on 15 August 1940. Produced from the boiling of household kitchen waste, this animal feed rapidly became nationally successful. Lord Morrison, a Labour MP for North Tottenham for twenty years, stands close behind her. Also present is the mayor, Alderman A.J. Lynch. Recollections of encounters with Tottenham Pudding are all fairly similar. One description by a local woman makes it clear: 'It didn't half stink,' she said, 'You could smell it all the way down to the High Road.'

Queen Mary passes Tottenham's salvage yard piggery. Humorously named 'Adolf's Kindergarten' the pigs had the dubious honour of tasting the new feed. Out of sight scores of schoolchildren enjoyed a grandstand view of Queen Mary by standing on top of the inclined roadway leading to the building known as the 'dust destructor'.

Elizabeth, the Queen Consort of George VI, inspects the Refuse Disposal and Salvage Works in Tottenham on 11 July 1940 accompanied by Lord Morrison who would, a few years later, be summoned to her daughter's coronation. Also on her visit to the borough Queen Elizabeth inspected the Women's Voluntary Service (WVS) centre and reviewed the Civil Defence Services at the Tottenham Polytechnic on the High Road. Throughout the war, a VIP visit, especially from royalty, often gave a much–needed boost to public morale.

Mr Leslie Burgin, the Minister of Supply, with twenty-two fellow MPs at the occasion of Tottenham's first Salvage Drive. This publicity opportunity demonstrated both the volume and the variety of materials it was possible to collect for recycling.

This national identity card was issued to local resident Reuben Ford of 15 Nelson Road in Tottenham. The National Registration Scheme was devised to safeguard the security of the nation. Everyone had to have an identity card and carry it with them at all times. As with ration books, the task of registering identity cards was overseen by the government's Food Office. Mr Ford was employed by the Tottenham and District Gas Co. He was also an area organiser for the Auxiliary Fire Service.

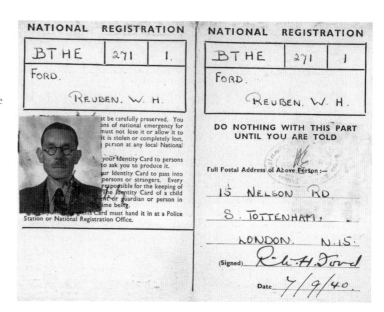

Mr Warren, a member of the staff at Bruce Castle Museum in Tottenham, stands between the blast walls of sandbags at the front entrance to the museum in May 1940. This was the only museum in the London area that did not close down at the outbreak of war. Visitors benefited from various exhibitions prepared for them and from the weekly cinema displays. The total number of visitors recorded for the year 1939/40 reached 41,302. Used jointly as a clinic and for local public displays about the war effort, the building also accommodated the RAF Barrage Balloon Squadron operating in the park.

The centre organiser, Alderman Mrs J.D. Lynch, and other WVS personnel checking household articles for sale in the lecture hall at Central Library in Tottenham High Road. Set up in 1938 at the request of Home Secretary Samuel Hoare, 1 million women were members countrywide by the end of 1941. The organisation of the National Savings in Tottenham owed its success to the WVS. From salvage drives and make-do and mend classes to supplying the Auxiliary Fire Service with mid-day meals or preparing parcels of craft work for disabled prisoners of war, the commitment of the WVS to the war effort in Haringey was second to none.

A trailer bearing a model of HMS *Hotspur*, 'Hero' class destroyer is displayed in the forecourt of Tottenham Polytechnic on Tottenham High Road. Adopted by Tottenham War Savings during Warship Week in March 1942, the target of close to three-quarters of a million pounds was an enormous sum of money. The crew of the *Hotspur* visited Tottenham in 1943 and were suitably honoured. The cost of the ship was finally paid for in 1948 when the vessel was decommissioned.

The Supermarine Spitfire sponsored by the Borough of Wood Green during the 'Wings for Victory' campaign. Synonymous with the Battle of Britain, the Spitfire remains the most potent symbol of Britain's finest hour. The Tottenham Savings Committee raised sufficient funds to cover the cost of twelve Lancaster bombers and forty-eight Spitfires. As a tribute to the people of each borough, the Ministry of Aircraft Production supplied a log-book in order that the operational activities of an adopted aircraft could be recorded.

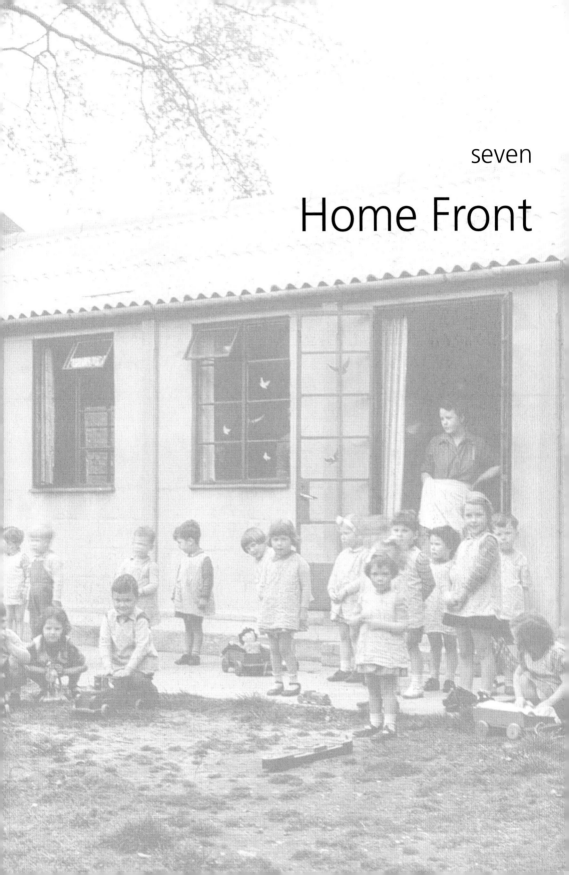

seven

Home Front

Officers of B Company 26th Middlesex Battalion Home Guard on their parade ground at Trinity School near St Michael's church in Wood Green in September 1944. Initially known as Local Defence Volunteers, the Home Guard were assigned the task of securing a major section of the River Lea in the event of an invasion – to keep it free from refugees and clear for military traffic.

Right: Home Guard Officer Arthur Smith of 26th Middlesex Battalion with his young daughter Monica who is seen here engagingly dressed like her father. During the day Mr Smith ran a newsagent shop at 13 Finsbury Road in Wood Green. Although somewhat derided as a 'Dad's Army', training for Home Guardsmen became decidedly intense as the war progressed with the growing possibility that they might, in all reality, soon be fighting alongside the regular army.

Opposite, below: Children at the Pembury House Day Nursery in Tottenham greet the camera with slight trepidation. Many day nurseries were adopted by one of the local services that agreed to keep them supplied with toys. Although most war work was initially voluntary, after 1941 it became necessary to conscript women particularly to supply the munitions factories with labour. Local authorities were therefore keen to reassure mothers that their children would be well looked after in their absence.

Staff of Bruce Castle Museum gather in the cellar for their second Christmas of the war. The lack of joviality may indicate just how much the war was beginning to take its toll. At the head of the table sits Captain Gordon the Commander of the Tottenham Home Guard. On his right is his son Tony and then Mrs Gordon, Mrs Smale and Mr Smale; to the right are Mrs Ware, Mrs Warren and Miss Warren.

The Civil Defence Committee and chief officers for Tottenham. Standing, from left to right, are: Cllr Pagin, Rees Williams (Borough Engineer), F. Davis (Borough Treasurer), Cllr Cox, Cllr Tyler, Alderman Morrell and Alderman Reid; seated from left to right are Mr Hamilton-Hogben (Ministry of Health in Tottenham), Cllr Mrs Irving, Alderman Field, Alderman Lord Morrison and E. Townson (Town Clerk).

Opposite, above: The lecture room at Tottenham town hall hosts a new clinic for mothers and children. The slogan on the blackboard, 'Health means Happiness', promotes a government-sponsored message of concern for personal healthcare. The economic depression of the 1930s had placed many residents in notable poverty and poor health was far from unusual. With wartime medical services increasingly stretched, information and guidance at a local level became an essential priority.

Opposite, below: Civil Defence Wardens' district centre headquarters in Marie House, from 1–3 Broad Lane, facing Page Green. The work of wardens was largely co-ordinated by the Borough Engineer. Rees Williams held the post in Tottenham and he organised the provision and training of people to carry out the task of rescuing victims of air-raids. He also managed the clear-up operation following the sounding of the 'all clear'.

Building operatives turn to face the camera while dining at St John's Hostel in Tottenham in 1945. A record of Civil Defence catering from 1939 to 1944 notes that the amount spent on a total of 983,230 meals came to £61,234 10s with most meals costing either one shilling or sixpence. The mobile canteen was present at most incidents and usually staffed by the WVS who would be fetched from home.

Opposite: This Air-Raid Precautions control map shows imaginary incidents for the purpose of training at the sub-control centre on the Paxton Road side of the Tottenham Hotspur football ground in February 1940. In operation all incidents were recorded but this, of course, did not reflect the total number of bombs dropped.

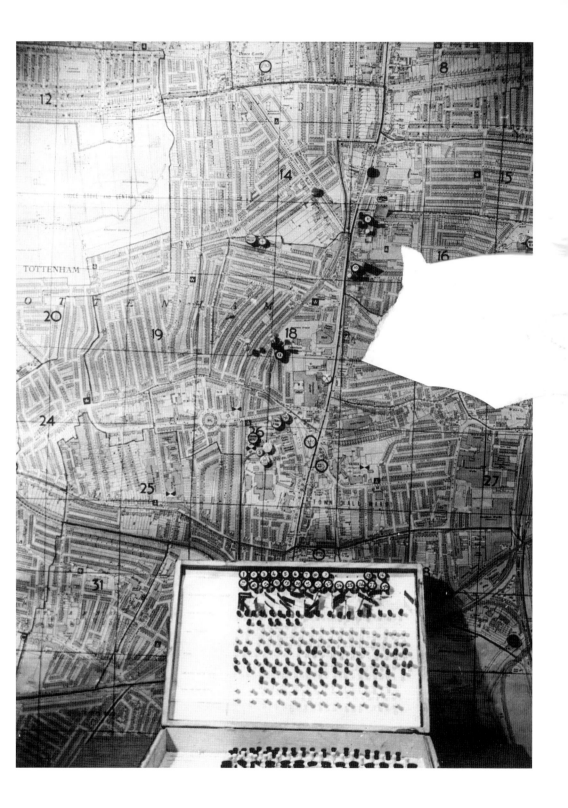

The Civil Defence heavy rescue squad with their vehicle in the yard of the Tottenham Lido Depot. Fifth from the left stands Victor Knott, an ex-Spurs player and former pupil of Lancasterian School in Tottenham. Amusingly the word 'heavy' appears to have applied not only to the work of the squad but also to the men themselves. The light-timber bedding provided for their use quickly proved unequal to normal wear and tear and cast-iron beds were then acquired to replace them.

Opposite, above: The Park View Civil Defence stores, displaying stacks of tin helmets, waterproof capes and trousers and uniforms. From left to right are: Mr Mundy – clearly disabled having lost a leg; Mr Marks, Mr Elkin and Mr White. A warden from Tottenham recalls: '…in the beginning I used to wear the full equipment, anti-gas equipment, cape and trousers – the whole lot. It was hard to get about. As time went by you dropped all that.'

Opposite, below: An Air-Raid Precautions exercise on the open space of Lordship Recreation Ground in Tottenham in 1939. Ambulances draw up before a row of dummy houses and administer the crew first aid to the 'victims' of a gas attack.

A view of the east side of Tottenham High Road showing the corner premises No.294 in use as Civil Defence Services headquarters for wardens, messengers and fireguards. The trees display sections that are painted white, indicating an access route for the National Fire Service. The fire station was on the west side of the road, out of view.

The new headquarters of 335 Tottenham company, 33rd Anti-Aircraft Battalion, Royal Engineers on Tottenham High Road, opposite Park Lane. This photograph formed part of a survey carried out by the Tottenham Camera Club working in association with Bruce Castle Museum during the early years of the war.

An ambulance driver, Mrs Woolmer, with her vehicle. The headlamps are almost completely covered for driving in the blackout although the stencilled letter 'A' would have been sufficiently illuminated to identify the vehicle status to other Civil Defence personnel. Although women drivers in Haringey did not always enjoy the full support of their male colleagues, many major incidents would have been much harder to handle without them.

BOROUGH OF HORNSEY

FORTIOR QUO PARATIOR

HOLIDAYS AT HOME
1944
PROGRAMME OF EVENTS

WEDNESDAY MAY 24-JUNE 30
FOR ADDITIONAL EVENTS SEE LOCAL PRESS
PRICE TWO PENCE

A holiday events programme for Hornsey in 1944. Such was the near impossibility of leaving both work and other wartime commitments that people were encouraged to enjoy a holiday at home; 'In other words sitting on a sandbag with your feet in a bucket of water,' as one woman quipped. A variety of sporting occasions, leisure facilities and entertainment events were provided for people to encourage relaxation. Cricket matches, boating on the lake at Alexandra Palace and dancing at the town hall are just three examples.

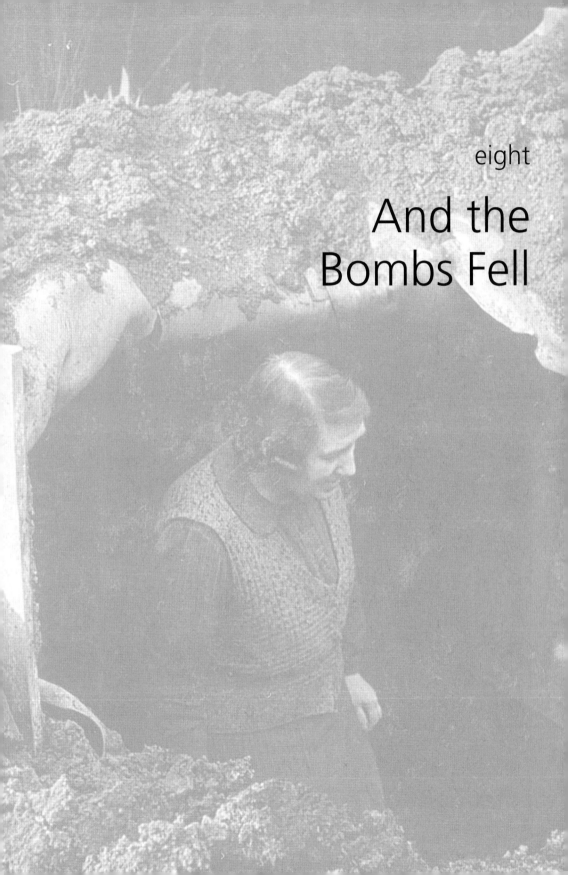

eight

And the Bombs Fell

"SPLINTERNET"

A SPECIALLY TREATED ADHESIVE FABRIC FOR WINDOW PROTECTION AGAINST BOMB BLAST

SPECIALLY SUITABLE FOR LARGE EXPANSES OF GLASS

MINIMUM LOSS OF LIGHT

DIRECTIONS FOR USE

Cut Fabric to desired length allowing for overlap on to the Window Frame. Moisten Glass with wet sponge. Apply Fabric to Glass, smooth down with wet sponge.

STOCKED IN 40 in. WIDTH

at **7**½ D. per yard

Obtainable at—

"HERALD" OFFICES, 825, HIGH ROAD, N.17.

Left: A local newspaper advertisement for a window covering with a curiously contemporary-sounding name was available from the *Tottenham Weekly Herald* newspaper offices. Such was the freak effect of the blast from exploding bombs that experiences differed greatly. One account describes a man whom, on hearing the sound of breaking glass, rushed outside to find his greenhouse curiously intact. In the morning, however, he saw that every window in the house had shattered.

Below: A view over Page Green Common, the site of the Seven Sisters trees (planted in 1928 and replaced several times since). It shows the houses of Ashmount Road on the south side and a typical trench shelter on the Green, later damaged by enemy action. On Lordship Recreation Ground another shelter of the same type known as the Downhill's Shelter was similarly destroyed, reportedly killing forty-one people and injuring many more. This tragic loss of life, even though greatly underestimated, gave increased urgency to the call for much deeper underground shelters. Subsequent research has placed the death toll far higher at around 150 people.

The view north west over the site of the former Reynardson's almshouses towards the Palace Theatre on Tottenham High Road. This photograph shows a static water dam and surface air-raid shelter used by the National Fire Service. The hut was used for training in dealing with incendiary bombs.

The Fire and First Aid Post at Dongola Road in Tottenham. The Auxiliary Fire Service was equipped with stirrup water pumps for their main task of rapidly tackling small-scale fires from incendiary bombs. By their ability to arrive quickly on the scene, these units were key players in preventing far worse devastation in Greater London. The National Fire Service was stretched to the limit during the Blitz and authorities realised to their cost the error of leaving the City of London largely devoid of the Auxiliary Fire Service.

A resident of Pelham Road in Wood Green inspects her Anderson Shelter unintentionally damaged by an Ack-Ack (anti-aircraft) shell.

A Civil Defence warden's post, annexe and trench shelter in the quadrangle of the Drapers' almshouses in Bruce Grove in 1945. The eternal dampness of the hurriedly constructed wardens' posts was a common complaint and in 1942 funds were made available to provide an annexe at each station for more tolerable sleeping accommodation. A warden recalls sleeping with a bell at the end of her bed tied to a string that could be pulled to wake her in an emergency.

Above: An unexploded 1,800kg bomb with the soubriquet 'Satan' is removed from a street in Wood Green. Just the size of the bomb casing was sufficiently terrifying. High-explosive bombs did not always explode but could nonetheless cause major impact damage to water and gas supplies.

Right: An arresting image of a young boy who stands facing the 250kg bomb, which dropped on the Gaumont Palace Cinema in Wood Green in November 1940; thankfully, it failed to explode.

Above: The enormous task faced by the Civil Defence is illustrated in this parade of defused enemy bombs. Each bomb has been given a nickname in reference to its size, shape or place of origin. During the Blitz the vast majority of bombs that were dropped were high explosive, incendiary or oil bombs. Diffusing unexploded bombs was a necessary but hazardous task undertaken by specialist units of the Bomb Disposal Squad.

Left: A bomb fails to explode upon hitting a hairdresser's shop at 308 High Road in Wood Green but nonetheless causes significant damage. A defiant notice from the proprietor and a hangman's noose below are displayed to the public, encapsulating the spirit of many Londoners during the Blitz.

Not far from Downhills Park, piles of rubble and bomb-damaged ruins show the effect of the first bomb of the war to hit Tottenham on Cornwall Road in late August 1940. Four years later a V1 flying bomb landed on almost the same spot on the exact same day of the same month. Civil Defence records note an occupied (indoor) Morrison shelter proved its worth on this second occasion by remaining intact as the building around it was demolished. It thus saved the lives of the occupants.

The emergency services rescue a casualty of a V1 flying bomb on Vincent Road in Wood Green in June 1944. The adjacent Coombe Road suffered similarly. The damage also spread to the nearby telephone exchange on Lordship Lane. As flying bombs flew in straight-line fashion, and were to some extent predictable, an Imminent Danger Warning System complete with klaxon hooters was devised to give a three-minute warning of a V1 approach. Fortunately the allied forces in France and Holland overran the missile launch sites and it was never necessary to put this scheme into operation in the borough.

A V1 flying bomb on Westbeech Road and Bury Road causes widespread devastation. One man remembers the enormous noise of a V1 over his school classroom: 'It was like an unsilenced motor cycle engine with a pulse... then the engine suddenly cut-out and we were told to lay on the floor... we heard the wind whistling over its wings. There was an enormous explosion – the whole air was full of dust... children screaming...' Although it was possible to destroy V1s in mid-air, their explosive power was such that fighter pilots were cautious not to get too close.

Devastation on Tetherdown at Fortis Green in Muswell Hill during 1944. A nearby resident recalls going to help: 'I looked around. The cinemas and the picture papers had so inured us that even at first glimpse it became ordinary. On the right a group of firemen were fighting a smouldering heap that covered Poultry Cottages... On the other side of the road the bomb had sliced away a wing of a modern three-story block of flats where light rescue men were already at work. Everywhere was order and swift action without any commotion.'

The Civil Defence message room at the control centre during a period of Red Alert in 1945. Notification of a current state of alert was via the telephone exchanges at Lordship Lane and Tottenham High Road where staff, on duty around the clock, would keep all the services and large employers informed of any change. The message room would continue to service teams who were working long hours dealing with specific incidents by dispatching motorcycle couriers with supplies.

Teachers and pupils of Tottenham Grammar School assemble for a school visit, each carrying their gas mask, c. 1942. On 15 March 1945 at 1.30 p.m., the last V2 rocket to reach Haringey hit waste ground at the end of Bull Lane close to the school. One boy did not hear the bomb explode but became suddenly aware that the air was full of bricks and slates and railings: '... all coming overhead as if in slow motion.' Directed by a teacher to help another boy who was badly injured, he took him by the arm only to discover it was almost severed inside the sleeve. The boy lost his arm but lived. Two other boys, however, lost their lives. They were Peter Goodman and Harold Poulton. As terrible as this incident was it could have been much worse. Had the rocket struck the school building directly, over 400 people would have died.

The wide impact of an exploding V2 rocket is all too apparent in this view of a badly scarred Tottenham Lane in Hornsey in 1945. Unlike the V1, or Doodlebug, these rockets could be launched from anywhere. Travelling at 3,600 miles per hour (four times the speed of sound) they could not be intercepted and arrived without warning. Seen here on the right a Barton's delivery van from Wood Green, although placed at the disposal of Civil Defence personnel, lends a sense of life carrying on regardless.

Medical aid point at Turnpike Lane underground station. During the Blitz it was often necessary to get away from all sights and sounds of the bombing if only for a relatively peaceful night's sleep. The tube provided a ready-made deep shelter underground where, contrary to popular assumption, people did not only sleep along the platform but also on boards and hammocks across the rails.

Right: At the rear of Bruce Castle Museum in Tottenham in the shadow of the north-west wing, Mr Warren of the museum staff talks with a member of the RAF barrage balloon unit stationed in the park.

Below: Barrage balloons were a common sight in Haringey as they were with the rest of London. Flying several hundred feet above the parks and open spaces, their purpose was to prevent enemy aircraft from conducting low-flying raids. Pilots knew to avoid them but they could also prove hazardous to people and property. Periodically winched down to be refilled and re-launched these enormous balloons could become un-tethered, leaving a 1,000ft of steel cable swinging around the rooftops. Until a balloon came to rest, very little could be done to stop it.

A boy from Woodlands Park School in Harringay being received at his evacuation home in Huntingdonshire in 1940. The wrench of leaving family was all too harsh as one woman remembers: 'It was a terrible morning. They went from Northumberland Park station but everyone met first at Coleraine School. They all had gas masks and their labels pinned onto their coats. My brothers were seven and eight years old. We didn't know where they were going. I think some of the children looked on it as an adventure. Some were crying but most thought they were going on their holidays.'

Evacuee Eunice Turner aged twelve (on the left) at Moat Farm in Tye Green in Essex, *c.* 1940. 'Tottenham High School, where I was due to go, was being evacuated to Saffron Walden and I didn't want to go there so I stayed on the farm where I was first sent. I went to school in the village and was taught by a retired teacher who was lovely but we did not learn much. I taught myself things because I loved reading. I was expected to help out on the farm. I did not mind doing things because everybody had to work – it was what you did.'

nine

Local Lives

Having served Britain during the First World War, Louis Klemantski lent his experience to the Second World War. A Jewish family of Polish descent, the Klemantskis lived in Brook House on Tottenham High Road – one of the great, lost houses of Haringey. After the war Louis returned to work as one of the principals of his family's firm, the Associated Wool Mills on the High Road.

Mr J.R.A. Lloyd of 42 Mannock Road in Wood Green. On joining the Civil Defence in 1938, he became an instructor prior to the declaration of war and held the post of Deputy Chief Warden for Tottenham until 1942. Mr Lloyd continued as one of the borough's four Civil Defence instructors after the war and was appointed Civil Defence Officer for Tottenham on 1 April 1951 when this photograph was taken.

KEEP THIS CARD SAFELY

NATIONAL SERVICE ACTS

Certificate of Registration in Register of Conscientious Objectors.

R.O. *London* Case No. *19778* Date *25. 1. 1945*

Holder's Name *Hawkes Herbert Granville*

Home Address *20 Linley Road Bruce Grove Tottenham N.17*

Date of Birth *24. 6. /19.07* Holder's Signature *H. G. Hawkes*

This is to certify that the above person by order of the competent Tribunal is—

*Delete alternatives before issue.

*(a) registered unconditionally in the Register of Conscientious Objectors.

*(b) registered conditionally in the Register of Conscientious Objectors.

*(c) registered in the Register of Conscientious Objectors as a person liable or prospectively liable to be called up for military service but to be employed only in non-combatant duties.

awStock

(Regional Controller, Ministry of Labour and National Service ... *L. S. E.* ... Region.)

READ THIS CAREFULLY.

Care should be taken not to lose this certificate, but in the event of loss application for a duplicate should be made to the nearest Office of the Ministry of Labour and National Service.

IF YOU CHANGE YOUR HOME ADDRESS OR YOUR NAME YOU MUST COMPLETE THE SPACE ON THE OTHER SIDE OF THIS CERTIFICATE AND POST IT AT ONCE. A new certificate will then be sent to you.

A person who uses or lends this certificate or allows it to be used by any other person with intent to deceive, renders himself liable to heavy penalties.

N.S. 62.   J1939 M16981/6093 9/44 3,000 D&Co. 40/1

A registration document carried by conscientious objector Herbert Hawkes of Linley Road in Bruce Grove in Tottenham. All conscientious objectors to the war were required to submit their reasons and have their case heard before a military tribunal. This card issued early in 1945 indicates conditions attached to his inclusion in the register, although evidence of Mr Hawkes' long-standing beliefs is clear if we consider the company he kept. Prior to the war, he spent the years with other pacifists undertaking different pastimes such as 'International Tramping Tours', where they enjoyed camping and walking in the countryside.

A studio portrait of Herbert Hawkes by the local photographer Andrée of 103 Bruce Grove in Tottenham, *c.* 1947.

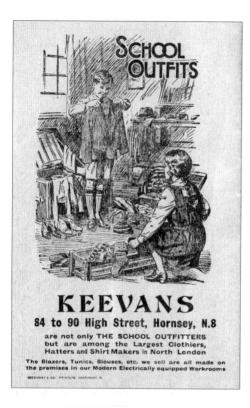

KEEVANS

84 to 90 High Street, Hornsey, N.8

are not only THE SCHOOL OUTFITTERS
but are among the Largest Clothiers,
Hatters and Shirt Makers in North London

The Blazers, Tunics, Blouses, etc. we sell are all made on
the premises in our Modern Electrically equipped Workrooms

GREENWAY & CO., PRINTERS, HARRINGAY, N.

This somewhat idealistic, although nonetheless charming, illustration from the back cover of the *Hornsey County School Magazine* from around 1943 contrasts sharply with contents of an inside page listing its former pupils killed fighting the war. Pupils mentioned are Frank Crook, Raymond Martin, Martin Moloney, Jack Ross and John Vizer. Full details of the circumstances of their deaths were made known to the school but they were not permitted for publication at the time.

E.R. Yescombe of Tottenham Public Libraries staff in full flying kit comprising thermal underwear, battle-dress uniform and a one-piece insulated flying suit with boots, gauntlets, flying helmet and goggles. As aircraft were unheated, flying in freezing temperatures was a serious matter. Boots were especially designed for the pilot to easily cut around the ankle to create a pair of shoes should he be forced to land on enemy territory.

Mirroring the same experience as Tottenham-born actor Leslie Phillips, Harry Pulfer expressed his preference for the Middlesex and Essex Regiments with the hope of being based reasonably close to home. He was promptly sent north to join the Durham Light Infantry. Harry served in the Middle East with the Eighth Army 'Desert Rats' and took part in the battle of El Alemein. Less than a week after D-Day he was sent to Normandy and fought his way through Belgium. Harry survived the war and was demobbed in 1945 shortly after sitting for this portrait in Berlin.

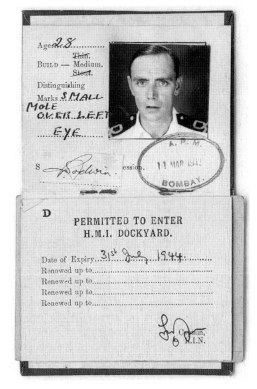

A Royal Navy Volunteer Reserve identity card issued to R. Godwin of Highweek Road in Tottenham, c. 1942. The card has been stamped at Bombay – a reminder that British forces were strengthened greatly by troops from Commonwealth countries, including India whose nationals fought in the Western Desert of North Africa and notably in Montecasino in Italy.

An oil painting of the interior of a warden's post by W.G. Woods, *c.* 1940. Being always ready and available at their post invariably meant long periods when there would be very little for Civil Defence wardens to do, often for many hours at a stretch. This painting by a local artist captures the boredom well and provides us with a sense of just how claustrophobic the building could become.

R.A. Searle, a schoolboy of 34 Seymour Avenue in Tottenham, kept an accurate log of bombing raids in a school exercise book. With lists of days, times and durations of raids, this private record gives us a picture of the growing intensity of air-raids affecting Haringey during the early years of the war. It also indicates just how important local Air-Raid Precautions proved to be.

TOTTENHAM AIR-RAID WARNINGS. (cont).

NO.	DAY.	TIME.	DATE.
4 5.	Friday.	5.58. P.M.	6TH September. 1940.
4 6.	Friday.	8.53. P.M.	6TH September. 1940.
4 7.	Friday.	11.32. P.M.	6TH September. 1940.
4 8.	Saturday	4.57. P.M.	7TH September. 1940.
4 9.	Saturday.	8.30. P.M.	7TH September. 1940.
5 0.	Sunday.	12.30. P.M.	8TH September. 1940.
5 1.	Sunday.	7.58. P.M.	8TH September. 1940.
5 2.	monday.	6.10. P.M.	9TH September. 1940.
5 3.	monday.	8.35. P.M.	9TH September. 1940.
5 4	Tuesday.	12.58. P.M.	10TH September. 1940.
5 5.	Tuesday.	4.0. P.M.	10TH September. 1940
5 6.	Tuesday.	5.22. P.M.	10TH September. 1940.
5 7.	Tuesday.	5.55. P.M.	10TH September. 1940.
5 8.	Tuesday.	8.13. P.M.	10TH September. 1940.
5 9.	Wednesday.	11.54. A.M.	11TH September. 1940.
6 0.	Wednesday.	3.20. P.M.	11TH September. 1940.
6 1.	Wednesday.	5.5. P.M.	11TH September. 1940.
6 2.	Wednesday.	8.40. P.M.	11TH September. 1940.
6 3.	Thursday.	4.45. P.M.	12TH September. 1940.
6 4.	Thursday	9.10. P.M.	12TH September. 1940.
6 5.	Friday.	7.35. A.M.	13TH September. 1940.
6 6.	Friday	9.45. A.M.	13TH September. 1940.

The widely recognised symbol of Tottenham Hotspur forms a majestic relief pattern on this wooden plaque which was presented to the *Grimsby Trawler* by the Football Club. This ship was requisitioned by the Ministry of Defence and converted for use as a minesweeper.

A concert party in Tottenham in 1944. Often many troops from overseas would be on leave in London and concert parties with songs and humorous sketches were provided for their entertainment. Wearing costumes made from Blackout curtains, Jo Dimmock and Joan Dunbar (in the centre of the back row) are flanked by their fellow players. Seated on the left at the front is Monica Smith, whose mother Marjory organised the entertainment for the troops.

Bruce Grove cinema in Tottenham during an April night in 1939. Improved technology in the production and projection of films had made cinema in the 1930s the most popular form of mass entertainment. An evening at the cinema would offer a stage show, cartoons, newsreels and two feature films. The potential of cinema as a propaganda tool was understandably exploited during the Second World War and films contained powerful messages. With carefully edited newsreels, an evening at the cinema could strengthen public resolve. A Haringey resident recalls what happened during the films if an air-raid occurred: '...they'd tell you and put up [on the screen] where the nearest shelter was but it was up to you whether you went out or not.'

Newly wedded couple Frank and Sylvia Fenton pose for the camera outside Christ Church on West Green Road in Tottenham in 1940. Despite the war or perhaps because of it many couples decided to tie the knot in a bid for a happy future. As staff members of Tottenham's public libraries they would have seen a growing increase in the demand for books and a continuation of this trend throughout the war. On hearing the air-raid siren, librarians were instructed to take the 'issue box' with them to the shelter in order to trace each book should a bomb destroy the library.

Above: Members of the Royal Electrical and Mechanical Engineers (REME) relax for a photograph. From left to right are: Craftsman Grange, Pte Green (fitter), Sgt Taffy Howard, Craftsman Chamberlain, Craftsman Phillips, Pte Selby (electrician) and Pte Slinn (coach trimmer).

Right: Private Arthur Green joined the REME. His war was spent in North Africa. Among other medals, he was awarded the Africa Star. Transported in July 1942 on the converted liner *Queen Elizabeth*, Arthur noted the sharp contrast between the officer's menu and the food served to other ranks. If he was given salt beef, potatoes and cabbage washed down with a cup of tea, the officers would be enjoying roasted lamb with mint sauce, potatoes and string beans followed by pudding marquise and coffee.

A carnival float passes through Wood Green displaying the words 'Thanks Mr Roosevelt' in December 1941. Dressed as the patriotic figure Britannia with the aid of an early twentieth–century brass fireman's helmet, Joan Dunbar salutes America's entry into the war against Germany and Italy. On 7 December, 360 aircraft from the Japanese air force had attacked the American Pacific Fleet at Pearl Harbour in Hawaii and a previously reluctant America entered the war.

Women workers at the Gestetner factory in Tottenham after the war. The increase in wartime production and shortage of labour meant women were conscripted to work in factories and to master supposedly masculine skills. A woman recollects her time at the Harris Lebus factory in Tottenham: 'We worked from seven o'clock in the morning until seven o'clock at night with one hour for lunch... Next to the factory was a slaughter-house – the sickening smell of horse flesh cooking used to waft through the canteen... The work was uninteresting... operating an electric saw and drilling machine... but the wages were good and we used to take the bus after work to Covent Garden and go dancing.'

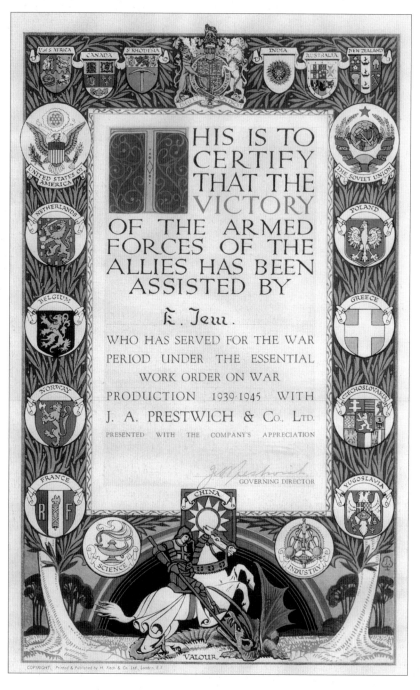

A colourful certificate presented by J.A. Prestwich & Co. to Mr E. Tew for serving his country through being engaged in essential war work. Based in Northumberland Park in Tottenham JAP engines were in use all over the world, largely for motorcycles. One of the more famous characters of the First World War, T.E. Lawrence, or Lawrence of Arabia, was killed in 1935 while riding a Brough Superior motorcycle fitted with a JAP engine.

ten

Victory and Peace

Left: Haringey residents join the Victory in Europe (VE) Day celebrations at Trafalgar Square in 1945. One woman poses for the camera colourfully attired in the national flags of Britain and the United States of America with the hammer and sickle of the Soviet Union embroidered on her velvet tunic. In contrast, the church of St Martin-in-the-Fields stands in the background offering a spiritual retreat from the festivities for those wishing to reflect on the war, give thanks to God and remember the dead.

Below: VE Day celebrations in Kolar in India in 1945. Frank Mitchell joined the RAF as ground crew during the war and was posted to India. He captures on camera the people of the southern India town of Kolar who were encouraged to join in the victory celebrations with allied troops. In pursuit of independence from British rule for many years, the Second World War had given India opportunity to renew their campaign. The last of the British armed forces withdrew at the end of February 1948.

Children are indulged by parents and neighbours alike as they celebrate with their own street party at Antill Road in Tottenham on VE Day in 1945. They would now grow up to enjoy the benefits of a long lasting peace in Europe.

A street party to celebrate VE day at Sutherland Road in Tottenham. Residents string-up bunting and gather for tea and cake to rejoice in the news of an end to the war in Europe. Happy memories are recalled: 'Everybody gave a bit. If you had a few currants or sultanas, whatever you had, a couple of spoonfuls of flour, everybody made it go a bit further. You contributed what you could.' Although hardship would continue for a number of years, for the first time in a generation they allowed themselves the thought of a brighter future.

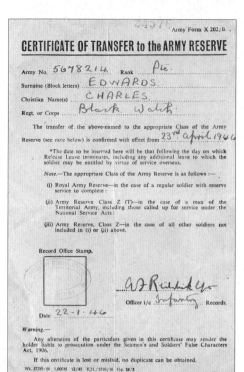

CERTIFICATE OF TRANSFER to the ARMY RESERVE

Army No. 5678214   Rank *Pte.*

Surname (Block letters) EDWARDS

Christian Name(s) CHARLES

Regt. or Corps Black Watch

The transfer of the above-named to the appropriate Class of the Army Reserve (see note below) is confirmed with effect from *23rd April 1946*

*The date to be inserted here will be that following the day on which Release Leave terminates, including any additional leave to which the soldier may be entitled by virtue of service overseas.

Note.—The appropriate Class of the Army Reserve is as follows :—

  (i) Royal Army Reserve—in the case of a regular soldier with reserve service to complete :

  (ii) Army Reserve, Class Z (T)—in the case of a man of the Territorial Army, including those called up for service under the National Service Acts :

  (iii) Army Reserve, Class Z—in the case of all other soldiers not included in (i) or (ii) above.

Record Office Stamp.

Officer i/c *Infantry* Records.

Date *22-1-46*

Warning.—

  Any alteration of the particulars given in this certificate may render the holder liable to prosecution under the Seamen's and Soldiers' False Characters Act, 1906.

  If this certificate is lost or mislaid, no duplicate can be obtained.

Wt. 37285/90 1,000M 12/45 KJL/1516/16 Gp. 38/3

Left: A certificate of transfer to the army reserve in 1946. Indicating an end to full-time military service, Charles Edwards, a private with the highly respected Black Watch Regiment, has his transfer form signed and stamped at the infantry office in Perth. The form indicates he was not a regular soldier prior to the war but was called up for active service.

Below: Civil Defence stand-down parade in front of the town hall in Tottenham High Road on 24 June 1945. Alderman Field presents the Clemens Cup for sport won by the Tottenham corps to the members of the Social and Sports Committee. From left to right are: Messrs Hardy, Lavender, Lower and Mead. Tony Mead held Warden's Post No. 30 and commanded much respect for the efficient execution of his duties throughout the war.

Members of the WVS wearing their distinctive green uniforms pass the saluting base at the Civil Defence stand-down parade on 24 June 1945. The Civil Defence Corps was disbanded but WVS continued to train and equip its members to meet the needs of emergencies in local communities. In 1966 the Queen awarded the WVS the honour of adding 'Royal' to its title. To commemorate the occasion, over 2,000 WRVS members attended a service in Westminster Abbey.

Borough of Tottenham.

VICTORY
THANKSGIVING SERVICE

IN

BRUCE CASTLE PARK,

ON

SUNDAY, 13th MAY, 1945.

The Service will be conducted by the
MAYOR'S CHAPLAIN
(Rev. F. J. Finch, M.A., Vicar of St. Ann's).

Order of Service.

Hymn : " O God, our help in ages past."

O GOD, our help in ages past,
Our hope for years to come,
Our shelter from the stormy blast,
And our eternal home.

Beneath the shadow of Thy Throne
Thy Saints have dwelt secure;
Sufficient is Thine Arm alone,
And our defence is sure.

Before the hills in order stood,
Or earth received her frame,
From everlasting Thou art God,
To endless years the Same.

A thousand ages in Thy sight
Are like an evening gone;
Short as the watch that ends the night
Before the rising sun.

Time, like an ever-rolling stream,
Bears all its sons away;
They fly forgotten, as a dream
Dies at the opening day.

O God, our help in ages past,
Our hope for years to come,
Be Thou our guard while troubles last,
And our eternal home.
Amen.

Opposite, below: A memorial plaque from the Tottenham and Edmonton Hebrew Congregation Synagogue in High Cross in Tottenham. Paid for by donations, this hand-painted metal plaque was placed on the interior wall of the synagogue as a memorial to David Brown, a member of the congregation killed in action on 29 June 1943. David would have gone to war knowing by heart the prayer of allegiance to the King that was carved in marble and mounted on the wall facing the congregation.

Left: A notice of a Victory Thanksgiving Service in Bruce Castle Park in Tottenham in 1945. Amidst the noise of celebrations of the Victory in Europe a more sombre occasion is scheduled to remember those whose future had been taken away from them by the war.

The Royal British Legion in Muswell Hill in 1948. This national charity founded after the First World War as a voice for the ex-service community began the process of looking to provide financial, social and emotional support to veterans and their dependants of the Second World War. The Muswell Hill branch notice board gives a clear indication of frequent activities and their purpose. Collectively the branches of the British Legion serve 13 million people each year throughout Britain and the Commonwealth.

Above: Lord Morrison, MP for Tottenham, attends the official opening of the Garden of Remembrance at Tottenham cemetery in 1952. People gather to take part in a service to honour those of the borough who have paid the ultimate sacrifice in the defence of their country.

D. BARNETT, *Esq.* -- £26. 5. 0.
FEDERATION of SYNAGOGUES. 26. 5. 0.
-. S. BROWN, £10. 10. 0.
In Loving Memory of
David Brown
killed in action 29th June 1943.
Age 21.

Evacuated for much of the war, children return home to a set routine of normal school activity. Schools mourned the loss of both teachers and pupils, and young male teachers were often notably conspicuous by their absence. The use of a news board in the classroom suggests that at last some news is positive.

An advertisement in the *Tottenham Weekly Herald* for the Royal Dance Hall on Tottenham High Road in1944. Although dancehalls suffered closures throughout the war, whenever there was an opportunity to go dancing it gave people a release from the mundane and a chance to mingle freely with the opposite sex. This trend continued well into the 1950s and a local woman recalls meeting her future husband there: 'I met Jim at The Royal. That was in 1954. We used to go dancing a couple of times a week. We got married in 1956.'

Above: A temporary building for the Bull Inn on Tottenham High Road, *c.* 1939. The original public house had become unsafe and was pulled down in 1938. With Air-Raid Precautions well underway the Borough Engineer would almost certainly have cast his eye over any unsafe building and made his recommendation. The Bull Inn was rebuilt in the post-war years and stands today with its new name, the Connaught Arms.

Opposite, below: A post-war view of Muswell Hill Broadway giving a picture of peacetime normality. Although rationing would continue until July 1954 all the visible signs of a borough at war have gone. Through inspired advertising the women of Haringey, along with the rest of the country, were soon to have their aspirations raised with the launch of the New Look by Christian Dior in 1947. Hungry for a touch of glamour, there would be no going back and high streets would increasingly respond to this trend.

Prefabricated houses or 'prefabs' were erected on White Hart Lane as part of the local authority's initiative to cope with the post-war housing shortage. A resident of Wood Green remembers the council allocating her and her husband a prefab: 'The rooms were quite big and we bought utility furniture from Times Furnishing in Wood Green. There was a toilet in the bathroom and the lounge doors opened onto the garden. It would be hot in the summer and cold in the winter but after ten years I was quite sorry to leave.'

A view of a cleared bomb-site at Stoneleigh South in 1947 with new bricks piled high in preparation for rebuilding. A landmine had dropped on this area on 18 September 1940. In addition to those destroyed, 130 houses were deemed unsafe. A fleet of lorries remained in operation for an entire weekend removing household furniture with improvised storage facilities found in the space under the stands at the Spurs' football ground.

Above: Coleridge Gardens was a former bomb site in Hornsey where landscaping now provides suitable space for relaxation. Marked efforts were made by the borough councils to heal unsightly scars caused by the recent hostilities.

Opposite, below: South Potteries in White Hart Lane in Tottenham. This successful family-run company which manufactured flowerpots had been a significant employer in the area during the 1920s and '30s with the business supplying nurseries of the Lea Valley. Like other local industries in the area, there was an enforced closure during the war years. Sadly, the post-war decline of the centuries-old Lea Valley nursery industry prevented a sustainable recovery for this business. The pottery carried on for some years but had to close in 1960.

A view of an area in Potters Bar in Hertfordshire where a housing estate is about to be constructed. Piles of broken concrete have been transported from Green Lanes in Haringey to be used for constructing the base course of new roads. In 1946 the government announced that Stevenage in Hertfordshire would become the first of a series of satellite, or new towns, to relieve London's post-war housing and over-crowding problems. For those residents of Haringey, displaced by the bombing, this offered an opportunity to make a new life for their families.

Index

Other local titles published by Tempus

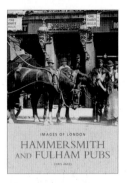

Hammersmith and Fulham Pubs
CHRIS AMIES

This volume offers an insight into the popularity and diverse role of pubs in Hammersmith and Fulham. Drawn from the collection held by The Hammersmith and Fulham Archives and Local History Centre, this selection of over 200 old images highlights a variety of architectural styles and past ways of life in this fascinating London borough during the past 130 years.
07524 3253 2

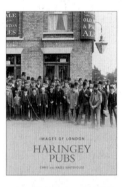

Haringey Pubs
CHRIS AND HAZEL WHITEHOUSE

This volume recalls the many varied roles pubs have played in the social life of Haringey during the last two centuries. Illustrated with over 170 old images each picture offers an insight into the popularity and changing role of Haringey's pubs – some of them still trading, others long since closed or demolished. This book is essential reading for all those interested in the history of Haringey and will bring back nostalgic memories of times past.
07524 3296 6

Tottenham Hotspur Football Club Since 1953
ROY BRAZIER

Over the last fifty years Tottenham Hotspur FC has enjoyed its fair share of highs and lows, including First Division Championship wins in 1950/51 and 1960/61 and FA Cup success on six occasions, including the double in 1960/61.

A follow-up volume to Tottenham Hotspur Football Club 1882-1952, this pictorial history recalls the players and managers who have helped Tottenham to success, and will appeal to anyone with an interest in the club.
07524 2924 8

London: Life in the Post-War Years
DOUGLAS WHITWORTH

These evocative images of London were taken in the years immediately following the Second World War (mainly 1945 to 1953) and are the work of Douglas Whitworth who took many photographs of people, places and events in the capital during this period. The pictures capture the atmosphere of the time, and also feature a succession of nostalgic views around some of London's most famous streets and landmarks, including Petticoat Lane and Speaker's Corner.
07524 2816 0

If you are interested in purchasing other books published by Tempus, or in case you have difficulty finding any Tempus books in your local bookshop, you can also place orders directly through our website

www.tempus-publishing.com